the Spirit is a-movin'

the spirit is a-movin'

R. Russell Bixler, Editor

CREATION HOUSE
CAROL STREAM, ILLINOIS

ISBN 0-88419-070-6
Library of Congress Catalog Card Number 74-12598

Contents

Part 6 The Holy Spirit Healing and Delivering

Part 7 The Holy Spirit Worshiping

Epilogue

Publisher's Foreword

God is moving by his Spirit,
Moving in all the earth,
Signs and wonders when God moveth—
Move, O Lord, in me.

That brief, reverent chorus expresses both the fact and the aspiration of the charismatic renewal in which it is often sung. The last third of the twentieth century is seeing particular supernatural activity, and millions of Christians pray that the great sweep of the Spirit will include them in real, individual, practical ways.

This is a book about the many arenas in which the Holy Spirit is active. If Christians agree on anything, it is that the Spirit cannot be limited to one point in a creed or one chapter called "Pneumatology" in a theology text. He is the living, breathing essence of God who establishes Christians in the faith, teaches them to love, empowers them to serve, guides their decisions, convicts the non-Christian, heals the sick, delivers the oppressed, causes men to worship truly...hence the table of contents.

The contributors to this book range from Baptists (James Moore, Frank Downing) to Catholics (Fr. Joseph Lange, Larry Tomczak) to Lutherans (Herbert Mjorud) to classic Pentecostals (James Beall) to Jews (Michael Esses). They include a variety of styles and approaches; the mixture is spiced with a delightful Scotsman (Thomas Smail), a Trinidadian (Winston Nunes), a medical doctor (Edward Atkinson), and an entertainer (Pat Boone).

All sixteen originally presented their material at the 1973 Greater Pittsburgh Charismatic Conference. Our special thanks go to R. Russell Bixler, chairman of the conference, who made the selections from the tapes and edited them for use in this book.

Part One

The Holy Spirit Establishing

1

The Center of Our Faith

James Lee Beall

Thank God that the Holy Spirit is God!

God the Holy Spirit came to fulfill the redemptive purposes of God in Jesus Christ, our Lord.

Let us declare some very important things that are the foundation with which everyone must come to grips.

First, we believe in the historical Jesus. We believe that at a point in time and space " . . . God sent forth his Son, made of a woman, made under the law, to redeem them that were under the law, . . . that we might receive the adoption of sons" (Galatians 4:4,5 King James Version).

The charismatic movement must continually realize that its roots are in the historical Jesus, even though we stress the contemporary Christ dwelling "in your hearts by faith; that ye, being rooted and grounded in love, may be able to comprehend with all saints what is the breadth, and length, and depth, and height; and to know the love of Christ, which passes knowledge, that ye might be filled with all the fulness of God" (Ephesians 3:17-19).

We believe in contemporary Christianity, the contem-

James Lee Beall is pastor of the large Bethesda Missionary Temple in Detroit. He has written three books and is also the speaker for a national radio program, "America to Your Knees."

porary Christ in the person of the Holy Spirit coming into our lives, taking up his dwelling place there. We believe that our bodies have become the temples of the Holy Spirit. "By one Spirit are we all baptized into one body, whether we be Jews or Gentiles, whether we be bond or free" (1 Corinthians 12:13). We have all been made to "eat the same spiritual meat; and . . . drink the same spiritual drink" (1 Corinthians 10:3,4).

We belong to Jesus Christ. As the Scripture says in Colossians 2:9,10, "For in him dwelleth all the fulness of the Godhead bodily. And ye are complete in him, which is the head of all principality and power." Our roots are in the historical Jesus. We have found him.

We believe in the historical gospel as Paul preached it. On the grounds of many infallible witnesses, we believe in the death, burial, and resurrection of the Lord Jesus Christ. We believe he was raised from the dead by the Spirit of holiness who dwelt in the Father. He was declared to be the Son of God by the resurrection from the dead. We further believe, according to Ephesians 4:8,9, that "when he ascended up on high, he led captivity captive, and gave gifts unto men. (Now that he ascended, what is it but that he also descended first into the lower parts of the earth?)" And when he ascended into the presence of God, as we read in Hebrews 1, God the Father said to our Lord, "Sit on my right hand, until I make thine enemies thy footstool."

Peter said that because of Jesus' ascension into the presence of God and his being seated at the right hand of God, "he hath shed forth this, which ye now see and hear" (Acts 2:33). Jesus went into the presence of God in heaven, walked into the true tabernacle not made with hands, and sprinkled everything in the heavens with his own blood so that grace and mercy might become the portion of his people. Then he prayed to the Father and said, "Send the promise of your Holy Spirit upon your people."

And God the Father sent the Holy Spirit—not only to fill

11

them, to enhance them, or to stir them up emotionally, but to invade their lives, to change people at the deepest possible level, to invade them inwardly, to move upon them, to make them people they could not possibly be.

We are rooted, we are grounded in the Scriptures. The charismatic renewal is not a theory up in the skies, something divorced from historic Christianity. We believe that we are the mainstream of Christianity. We believe that we are getting things together that should have been together for a long while.

Please note that when we come in the Scriptures to articulate things about the Holy Spirit we are dealing with personal pronouns—not a nebulous something, not an ethereal force, not a generality, not a great God in the great somewhere. The Holy Spirit is a person! "When *he* is come, *he* will reprove the world of sin, and of righteousness, and of judgment" (John 16:8).

When we say the Holy Spirit dwells within us and our bodies have become the temples of the Holy Spirit, this is synonymous with the term "Christ in you, the hope of glory."

Jesus said, "If ye abide in me, and my words abide in you, ye shall ask what ye will, and it shall be done unto you" (John 15:7). He said that when the Holy Spirit comes to a person, "My Father will love him, and we will come unto him, and make our abode with him" (John 14:23). So we are not slighting the Father or the Son when we are dealing with the Holy Spirit. We are dealing with the family, the triunity of God. When we deal with the Holy Spirit, it is God in his fullness who is coming to take up his abode within us, to influence us in every possible way.

When we are dealing with the Holy Spirit, we are dealing with the most psychologically sound force in the universe, because we are dealing with God. He comes in primarily to stimulate us. When the Holy Spirit comes, he comes with divine strength, applying that strength to our inner lives. Where does he apply it? He applies it intellectually, emotionally, spiritually, volitionally. He touches the total man. If we do not have the Holy Spirit touching the total man, we become lopsided, off-balance. We are not interested in that.

But there is somebody I want to emulate. There is someone whom I would like to be like in every detail, and that is the Lord Jesus Christ. The Holy Spirit dwelt within him in totality, in fullness. The Spirit of the Godhead bodily dwelt within him and made him the most balanced, poised, sane, strong, sensible individual that ever walked on the face of the earth. And if the Holy Spirit made Jesus that kind of person, we can be safe in his hands.

When the Holy Spirit comes, he stimulates your natural forces and talents. He does not make you a cipher, a nothing, a zero. He takes you as a person. He redeems people with names and personalities; we retain our individualities and eccentricities. We retain the things that make us oddly us.

Religion too long has tried to regiment all of us, to make us look the same, act the same, talk the same. We don't want that. Thank God we can have the work of the Holy Spirit, God's redemption, and retain our personalities. One of the greatest aspects in the whole charismatic picture is "You are the body of Christ, and members in particular" (1 Corinthians 12:27). God has given gifts to all of us as members of the Body of Christ, all of us with gifts differing, with personalities differing, with insights differing—yet we make up one Body.

The Lord stimulates you into life. He stimulates you into reading the Scriptures, into prayer, into real hunger. He enhances you. He stimulates the realm of your will.

"When He comes," Jesus said, "the Holy Spirit will not speak of himself but will make somebody else the center of everything."

It is very important that all of us realize that we must proceed from a center. If you are off-center, you know what happens. You become lopsided, unbalanced, strange. The only way we can have balance is by having the right center.

Somebody has got to be in the center. The center of our faith is not a thing. It is a somebody. The center of our faith is not a doctrine. It is not a creed. Doctrines and teachings are important; if you believe wrong, you fall into a ditch. If you are a blind leader of the blind, you all fall into a ditch. But although it is important what we believe, that is not the center of our faith. The center is Jesus Christ the Lord.

If you do not start with the right center, you end up with wrong conclusions. Centuries ago, men thought the earth was the center of our solar system. They were wrong. Finally they came to grips with the fact that the sun is the center of our solar system.

When a person gets off-balance, we say he is eccentric or egocentric—he has put himself in the center of his world. That is easy to do when you first become involved in charismatic things. "The Holy Spirit! What is he going to do with *me?*" The dreams begin.

One of the scriptures I learned early in life is Hebrews 10:35,36—"Cast not away therefore your confidence, which hath great recompence of reward. For ye have need of patience . . . ." I don't want to be patient. God says, "Be patient. Take it easy. Cool it."

For ye have need of patience, that, after ye have done the will of God, ye might receive the promise.

For yet a little while, and he that shall come will come, and will not tarry.

Now the just shall live by faith: but if any man draw back, my soul shall have no pleasure in him.

But we are not of them who draw back unto perdition; but of them that believe to the saving of the soul (Hebrews 10:36-39).

We must get the center straight. Jesus is the center of everything. And we don't need to coach him.

Historically, there have been some shifts away from the center. The early Church, after about three hundred years, began to shift its center to the realm of ecclesiastical religion until Jesus Christ was replaced by area bishops at the center of the faith. Eventually the Roman pontiff became the center of the Christian faith. After a while the Reformers came along—Luther, Calvin, Knox, and all the others—and they shifted the center to the Bible. Our creed became the center of Christianity, the center of our fellowship.

We are a part of a charismatic movement, and it is a movement toward something. Thank God it is a movement toward the center, Jesus Christ. He is more to us now than he has ever been in all our lives.

Again I repeat: when the Holy Spirit comes, he does not speak of himself. He speaks of Jesus.

One of the by-roads that many people get into when they receive the baptism in the Holy Spirit is that they begin to deal exclusively with future things. When our Center is the Lord Jesus Christ, we find that the Holy Spirit deals primarily with the present before he deals with the future. He deals with us where we live.

The Holy Spirit was sent to us not just to make life easier, to give us extraneous things. He did not come to make us comfortable. When we first receive the baptism, there is exuberance, joy, acceleration. But then we find that he begins to nudge us, to send barbs our way, until before long he is inciting certain emotional responses that we have not wanted. We begin to see that very often after our highest moments we have some of the deepest problems with ourselves.

Over the years, I haven't found God changing the world around to suit me. Instead, he begins to work in me, to change me. God is going to make something out of me if it kills me! He is out for character. He is going to make me a person with whom he can live eternally. He is working by the Holy Spirit to make real character so he can live with me, so I can live with myself, and so other people can live with me.

Jesus Christ becomes the center of our faith by the activity

15

of the Holy Spirit, and his central purpose is the development of character. "He which hath begun a good work in you will perform it until the day of Jesus Christ" (Philippians 1:6). You don't need other people to tell you that changes are taking place. You know you are mellowing. Things are happening, and they are good.

The third thing to determine is that God gave you the Holy Spirit as this final, beautiful conclusion that he is for you. If God is for you, just have the simple faith to say, "God's for me." Have the presence of mind to let him bless you. Stop running around like a chicken with its head cut off. Settle down and let him bless you. If God is for you, who can be against you?

When Jesus first called his twelve disciples, he called them not primarily to be ministers (that was secondary), not only to heal the sick (that was secondary), not only to cast out demons (that was secondary), not only to preach the Kingdom of Heaven (that was secondary). The primary purpose of calling the disciples was *for them to be with him* (Mark 3:14).

That is why the Holy Spirit is given to us—to bring us into intimate union with Jesus Christ. We are with him, but not only with him; he is in us. This is the most intimate union possible.

But we get involved in ministry, in counseling, in preaching, in the activities of the church—and after awhile the prime consideration of our total life has taken a back seat. Instead of being with Jesus and having that intimacy continue, we have allowed other things to take the center.

What is the charismatic movement about? It is about Jesus.

I do not believe the established church will ever be the same. I don't think it will even be able to return to the status quo of five to eight years ago. "This is the day which the Lord hath made; we will rejoice and be glad in it" (Psalm 118:24)! Years ago a Swedish pastor from Stockholm came to our church in Detroit. In broken English he said, "Our winters are long in Sweden. Great deal of snow and a lot of ice. Every year in our history we have experienced spring. Spring comes, and we look forward to spring after our long winters every year. But every time spring comes, we have a lot of problems with spring. The snow melts, the ice melts, the rivers fill, the fields are flooded, cattle drown, fences are washed out, acres of farmland are destroyed. But we still want spring."

That is the way God's visitation is. It washes out a lot of fences. Denominational boundaries get swept away. Some people even drown in the process! A lot of farms are never the same as they were.

Thank God for his patience with us! Thank God for the patience of Jesus!

Go to "Jerusalem" in your real world, in a real city, and wait there until you are endued with power. That power will not make you a prognosticator, but it will make you a witness of Jesus Christ "to the uttermost part of the earth."

2

The Head of the Church

James Hodges

David du Plessis, God's world ambassador for Pentecost, tells of going to Scotland and asking the church authorities there, "Who is the head of your church?"

They answered, "Jesus Christ."

And he said, "Good, I'm a Presbyterian."

He went to Germany and asked a Lutheran, "Who's the head of your church?"

The answer was "Jesus Christ."

Du Plessis said, "Good, I'm a Lutheran."

He went to England and asked the Anglicans who was the head of their church, and they said, "Jesus Christ."

And he said, "Well, I guess I'm an Anglican."

Then he went to Rome and asked who was the head of the Catholic church, and they said, "Jesus Christ."

And Brother David said, "Good, I'm a Catholic."

Ephesians 1:19-22 describes the true Head of the Church,

James Hodges, a graduate of Wheaton College and Central Baptist Seminary, is an American Baptist minister. After several pastorates, he joined the faculty of Christ for the Nations Institute in Dallas in 1972.

the Lord Jesus Christ. Paul wants us to know

> what is the exceeding greatness of his power to us-ward who
> believe, according to the working of his mighty power,
> Which he wrought in Christ, when he raised him from the
> dead, and set him at his own right hand in the heavenly places,
> Far above all principality, and power, and might, and
> dominion, and every name that is named, not only in this world,
> but also in that which is to come:
> And hath put all things under his feet, and gave him to be the
> head over all things to the church (King James Version).

The Head of the Church is the Lord Jesus Christ—not a man, not a hierarchy.

Paul says he is the resurrected, ascended, exalted, glorified Son of God. He is the Head, and as Head he is "far above all"—far above principalities and powers, far above all satanic power. He is over every name, not only in this material world, but also in the spiritual, eternal world. Hebrews 6 talks about "the powers of the world to come." The world to come is the eternal world, the spiritual world of God which has already invaded our sinful world, but which will continue forever in eternity.

When our Lord stood before Pontius Pilate, he was quizzed a little and was reluctant to answer. But one of the statements Jesus did make was, "Thou couldest have no power at all against me, except it were given thee from above" (John 19:11). Jesus was crucified, but the Kingdom of Jesus won out over the kingdom of Pilate! Early Christians were thrown into the arena with lions, but who won out? Rome or Christ? Christ won!

Jesus is the Head of all things, and we are connected to him because he is our Head and we are his Body. That puts us over all things—but one of the most frustrating things is that Christians often don't act as though they are God's people.

I was walking down the hall in the Pittsburgh airport recently when suddenly I heard beautiful music, heavenly music—right there in the airport. I thought I'd missed the Rapture, so beautiful it was. Somewhere people were singing, "God be with you till we meet again . . . ."

I looked around, and over in the corner at the last gate stood a group of people sending off a missionary. They were unashamed. They were God's people sending off a member of the Family. It changed the whole atmosphere.

We are God's people, made to praise the Lord. We belong to the Lord Jesus Christ, who is the Head of the Church. Our problem is not theological acknowledgment that Jesus is the Head. Our problem is holding onto the Head.

The second chapter of Colossians tells us,

> Ye are complete in him, which is the head of all principality and power:
> In whom also ye are circumcised with the circumcision made without hands, in putting off the body of the sins of the flesh by the circumcision of Christ:
> Buried with him in baptism, wherein also ye are risen with him through the faith of the operation of God, who hath raised him from the dead.
> And you, being dead in your sins and the uncircumcision of your flesh, hath he quickened together with him, having forgiven you all trespasses;
> Blotting out the handwriting of ordinances that was against us, which was contrary to us, and took it out of the way, nailing it to his cross;
> And having spoiled principalities and powers, he made a shew of them openly, triumphing over them in it.
> Let no man therefore judge you in meat, or in drink, or in respect of a holyday, or of the new moon, or of the sabbath days:
> Which are a shadow of things to come; but the body is of Christ.
> Let no man beguile you of your reward in a voluntary humility and worshipping of angels, intruding into those things which he hath not seen, vainly puffed up by his fleshly mind,
> And not holding the Head, from which all the body by joints and bands having nourishment ministered, and knit together, increaseth with the increase of God.
> Wherefore if ye be dead with Christ from the rudiments of the

world, why, as though living in the world, are ye subject to ordinances,

(Touch not; taste not; handle not;

Which are all to perish with the using;) after the commandments and doctrines of men?

Which things have indeed a shew of wisdom in will-worship, and humility, and neglecting of the body; not in any honour to the satisfying of the flesh.

Everybody is holding onto something, whether he is a Christian or not. Believers in Jesus, members of his Body, are always to be holding onto him, our Head, not merely saying theologically that Jesus is the Head of the Church, but holding onto the Head by faith. It is not that God will let you go, nor that you have to hold on and struggle until the end. God is going to make it to the end, and we are going to make it too because we are in Christ. But in our dynamic, daily experience, in the life of the Church, in our individual hearts, in the corporate structure, we must hold onto the Head.

The problems in Colosse were not only unbelief and wrong doctrine, but also the fact that believers were holding onto something other than the Head. They held onto laws and ordinances.

I do not advocate lawlessness. God forbid! But the problem is that some of us have substituted laws and ordinances for the Head. You may know somebody who says his religion is the Ten Commandments. I usually say to these folks, "Well, that's too bad, because all of us have broken the Ten Commandments." God obviously is not calling us into lawlessness, and certainly the obedience and submissiveness in the Body of Christ which we are hearing so much about today is not just an obligation to fulfill some outward law; it is our loving response to the Lord, the Head of the Church. He has written his law in the hearts of his Church. Most of the religions of the world have moral and ethical principles comparable to the Ten Commandments. Therefore their followers are under laws and ordinances.

Jesus did say, "If you love me, keep my commandments." But the main commandment of our Lord is to love one another. Love does not envy or covet. We simply can't obey unless we are drawing ability from the Head, our Lord Jesus Christ. Once you sever the Body from the Head, there is no life, although the Body might clutch or hold onto things despite the fact that it is severed. We must draw power and ability from the Head.

Paul says the laws and ordinances served their purpose, but they were only a shadow of what was to come. Once the substance comes, there is no longer any need for the shadow. If I have Jesus, I no longer strive to keep the laws and ordinances. I simply submit to my Lord, who never broke any of these laws. He has written them on my heart, and as I draw ability from him, he helps me to keep the command-ments of God.

One thing which causes a lack of joy in some Christians is the fact that they are laboriously trying to keep laws. They are in a constant, dismal struggle, but they have little awareness of the Head. Paul says the Lord blotted out the ordinances. These laws were against us, contrary to us, and he took them out of the way, nailing them to his Cross. He removed the condemnation, the penalty of the law. He took it all out of the way at Calvary.

But some Christians remain caught in this trap. Obeying rules is the summit of their relationship to God. It only brings them into bondage. Jesus said, "Come unto me, all ye that labour and are heavy laden, and I will give you rest. Take my yoke upon you, and learn of me; for I am meek and lowly in heart: and ye shall find rest unto your souls. For my yoke is easy, and my burden is light" (Matthew 11:28-30). When Jesus gave this invitation, he was across the street from the Temple. He saw people coming day after day, bound in duty and obligation and law-keeping. They were under a heavy yoke. The yoke of Jesus is light. The yoke we humans put on people is heavy.

The Colossians were also holding onto tradition. Tradition is not all bad nor all wrong, but when tradition supersedes the Word of God, it becomes sin.

The traditions Paul mentions included the business of diet. "Let no man therefore judge you in meat, or in drink," he warns.

". . . Or in respect of a holyday." As a Baptist, I held Sunday in such legalistic bondage that I couldn't enjoy Sunday. (I'm not saying that Sunday isn't the Lord's Day; *every* day is the Lord's day.) But I was under such bondage before the Lord freed me that I got up-tight if my wife wanted to wash out a diaper on Sunday! Paul says not to be brought into condemnation over any of these things, because we are not to hold onto any of them. They only have meaning when we are correctly related to the Head, the Lord Jesus Christ.

"Let no man beguile you of your reward in a voluntary humility and worshipping of angels." I believe in angels. Angels rejoiced when we were saved. An angel was assigned to you when you were born. Jesus talks about children having angels, and I know that when you grow up you don't lose your angel. Praise God! But there is a subtle danger. Right now there is a fast-growing belief that Jesus is the Archangel Michael. And if we are not careful, we can be deceived. Our spiritual experiences must be in line with the word of God.

A very prominent Full Gospel Business Man was trying to pray about some matters, and he said to his wife, "Now you won't hear from me until I hear from God." So he went to a motel, locked himself in, and prayed and fasted for three days. On the third day, as he was in prayer and supplication, all of a sudden a beautiful figure appeared in his room. He said his first thought was to bow down and worship. As he started to kneel, there was something inside him that held him back, and he said to the angel, "Identify yourself in the name of Jesus."

The angel said, "Satan."

The man said, "You'll have to leave," and so the devil left. Had it been an angel of God, God would never have been displeased by the man's demand that he identify himself. Confirmation is necessary, because Satan can make himself appear as an angel of light.

This relates to the problem in the Colossian church; they were caught up in gnosticism, which was the denial of the humanity of Jesus.

There have been two errors that have always plagued the Church—two errors that Satan tries to perpetuate. One denies the deity of Jesus; the other denies his humanity. These thoughts are around us today. Those who have come out of liberal traditions, never really believing in the divinity of Christ, suddenly find Jesus and discover that they have been washed in the blood, and they get all excited. Then Satan tries to get them off on a tangent, and they tend to go to the other extreme and almost deny the humanity of Jesus. Watch out for this. Every spirit has to be measured by God's Word. In Colosse they were losing their hold on the Head as they were caught up in mysticism and gnosticism. Remember that the Holy Spirit never says anything contradictory to the Word, because he authored the Word.

Another thing the Colossians were holding onto besides the Head was doctrine. By doctrine I mean teaching, and I am not minimizing the importance of it. But for some people, Christianity is a system of religious symbols and theological concepts. The right words are to be said and the right thoughts are to be thought. But as important as doctrines and teachings are, they themselves are not reality; they are simply descriptions of reality.

In Colosse there were some who were dogmatically holding to some description of religion, and in doing so they were excluding those who did not hold to their version. There is danger in this also. I used to think that Baptists had a corner on truth. Back in seminary I was God's defender; if God got into trouble, I had to help him. I fought the liberals who didn't believe in the resurrection and the virgin birth and all that. Then I realized that I wasn't ministering to the liberals; I was just holding dogmatically to some descriptions I had. I was in almost as bad a shape as they were.

The reality is Christ! The Body is of Christ, and these descriptions are important, but we must not let them supersede the reality himself, the Lord Jesus Christ.

I praise God that in today's move of the Spirit there is a merging of word and deed. God's revelation comes through his mighty arm, but it comes also through the Word of God. It has merged the good emphasis of fundamentalism, believing the Word of God to be objectively true, and the good emphasis of neo-orthodoxy, which says God's revelation is bigger than a page.

Jesus said, "This Gospel of the kingdom shall be preached in all the world for a witness unto all nations; and then shall the end come" (Matthew 24:14). I believe we are seeing an ever-increasing power in the gospel as it is preached around the world. It used to take ten years to win one Moslem to Christ; now there are an estimated seven million Indonesians who are born-again, baptized, Spirit-filled believers—and this has happened in just a short while. How do you explain it? It is the moving of the power of God, the merging of word and deed.

First Peter 2 says,

Unto you therefore which believe he is precious: but unto them which be disobedient, the stone which the builders disallowed, the same is made the head of the corner,

And a stone of stumbling, and a rock of offence, even to them which stumble at the word, being disobedient: whereunto also they were appointed.

But ye are a chosen generation, a royal priesthood, a holy nation, a peculiar people; that ye should shew forth the praises of him who hath called you out of darkness into his marvellous light.

The Jewish builders disallowed Jesus, but so it often is today. Sometimes Gentile church builders disallow Jesus' headship also. Nevertheless, he is the cornerstone, the chief stone.

For the husband is the head of the wife, even as Christ is the head of the church: and he is the saviour of the body.

Therefore as the church is subject unto Christ, so let the wives be to their own husbands in everything.

Husbands, love your wives, even as Christ also loved the church, and gave himself for it;

That he might sanctify and cleanse it with the washing of water by the word,

That he might present it to himself a glorious church, not having spot, or wrinkle, or any such thing, but that it should be holy and without blemish (Ephesians 5:23-27).

Jesus loved the Church and gave himself up for the Church.

In the present ministry of Christ, we see that he is doing two things basically related to each other. He is sanctifying and he is cleansing. The Lord is going to present to himself a glorious Church without wrinkle, and it will be holy. He is cleansing the Church with the washing of the water by the Word of God.

The greatest thing going on as far as I am concerned is the impartation and receiving of the Word of God. (When I was in seminary, we read books about books about the books of the Bible, but we seldom got around to reading the Bible! We had one class on Ephesians in Greek. That was rich; that fed me.) God, by our reading and studying of the Word, is cleansing and purifying his people.

By the moving of his Spirit and the revelation of his Word, God in this hour is removing some strange bedfellows from the Church. One of them is dispensationalism, which says that the gifts of the Spirit died when John died around 90 A.D. Another strange bedfellow is the occult. Another is liberalism. Praise the Lord, the tide is turning today. The tide has turned. The movement is from God. It is not dying out; it is getting swifter in current and deeper in depth.

Proclamation of the Word of God brings purification, which leads to restoration. Restoration is beginning to do what God's Word said we should have been doing all along but have not been doing. As the Head, he is sanctifying and cleansing his Church. We are getting together by his power. As the last Adam, he is the Head of a new race. Jesus is the Head of a redeemed race, his Body, the Church.

Jesus is the Head, whether you are Lutheran, Presbyterian, Baptist, independent, or renegade. If you are born again, if you know the Lord, you are in his Church, and he is the Head. Hold onto him.

Part Two

The Holy Spirit Loving

3

The Christian Community
—Maturing in Love

Fr. Joseph Lange

What is it like to live in a Christian community?

God has revealed his secret plan to us, Paul says in Ephesians. That plan is that we all should be joined to Christ.

We are born of the flesh—born into isolation, aloneness. As we grow up, we find we are not really communicating with others and others are not communicating with us. This builds up an insecurity, a distrust of one another that leads to all kinds of hang-ups.

The world solves the problems of people living in the flesh by demanding external conformity. This is the world of law, of good manners, of customs, of conforming to certain patterns. When people do this, they experience a kind of peace—the peace which the world gives.

The world defines goodness in these kinds of external

Fr. Joseph Lange is the founder and director of the Center for Renewal in Allentown, Pennsylvania. A graduate of Niagara University (B.S.), Catholic University (M.S.), and the University of Chicago (M.A.), he is a former hospital chaplain, parish priest, and college instructor. He has written one book and numerous articles; he also serves on the advisory committee of the National Catholic Charismatic Service Committee.

terms: you are a good person if you are like everybody else; evil is not conforming.

The good news is that the Father sent the Son, and together they sent the Spirit to let each man know that he is totally known and totally loved. If he accepts that, he is saved from his aloneness. If he accepts a personal relationship with the Father and the Son, he is saved from his aloneness through the power of the Spirit; he is redeemed from his isolation and brought into communication with the living God.

Genesis describes man as having a very close relationship with God, walking with him in peace in the garden. The fundamental message is that man was meant to live in a personal, peaceful relationship with God. To be saved is to be brought into that relationship. Then, because we are set free from our insecurities through knowing that God loves us, we don't care so much about what other people think. We are free to love others. And besides that, we share in the very life of God himself—we share in his Spirit, who gives the power to know ourselves and others as God does, and the power to love ourselves and others as God does. Never again do we have to fear that we cannot be loving persons. We know we have that God-given power to love.

The difference between being good in the eyes of the world by conforming to external things and being touched by God's love is that God's love is transforming. It says, "I take you right where you are. You don't have to be good before I love you. You don't have to change yourself before I find you acceptable. I love you just as you are." Being accepted that way sets all sorts of things free in us. We behave differently externally, but the change begins on the inside. The prophecies of the Old Testament said God would pour out his Spirit to change our hearts of stone to hearts of flesh. That means we are going to become lovers. Everything that has to do with the New Covenant has to do with the heart—not with external standards.

The community of the faithful, each of whom is individually touched by the saving presence and love of a personal Savior, has been set free to love each other. They have found the peace Christ gives—which is being right with themselves, right with their neighbor, and right with the Lord. That peace is in their hearts. As we live together in that kind of way, we enter the Kingdom which Jesus talked about so much. We become the Body of Christ. We are joined to him, the Head. We share his life and his Spirit, who raised him from the dead.

When we first accept Jesus, we say, "Jesus, take over my whole life." But when somebody says, "Hey, how about a lift home?" we say, "Sorry, brother, I'm not going that way." It's like the fellow who writes a love note, "Oh, my darling, I love you so much. For you I would climb the highest mountain, swim the deepest river, fight the most ferocious beast. Yours forever, Jim.

"P.S. I'll see you this weekend if it doesn't rain."

It's one thing to make a glowing commitment, but it's another to translate it into the nitty-gritty of daily life. Each time we are confronted with the choice of turning this or that area of our life over to the Lord, we are confronted with the necessity of dying to our self-centeredness, our pride, our desire to have our own way and to let go so we can come to new life.

On Death and Dying is a book by E. K. Ross, a psychiatrist who interviewed hospital patients who had been told they were going to die. She learned that there are five steps they go through.

The first is denial. It is practically impossible to believe in our own personal death.

The second stage is anger, a general form of anger, unfocused, unlocalized.

The third stage is compromise.

The fourth stage is confusion and sometimes depression.

Finally comes acceptance.

That book reminded me that Scripture has often seen a very close tie between sin and death. If we look at what it means for us to die to our self-centeredness, to wanting our own way, and to accept God's direction in our lives, we see that we go through the same stages. We hear the gospel, the challenge of dying to ourselves, but our reaction is, "That can't mean me." The next step is generally one of anger. Then comes compromise. (Remember Saint Augustine: "Lord, make me pure, but not yet.") Finally, with acceptance comes new life and peace.

As you begin to turn your life over to the Lord step by step, you find that each time it is deeply rewarding. It always brings more light, more peace, deeper joy. And gradually you learn to let go.

The Body of Christ is meant to be the Messianic presence. When Jesus was on earth, the presence of the Messiah was in him, but now it is spread out through the whole Body. People encountering that Body of Christ are meant to encounter the living, saving presence of the Messiah. All his power, all his life, all his forgiveness, all his healing are meant to be encountered within the living Christian community, the Body of Christ.

How do you get into the Body of Christ? We all know you have to be baptized and believe. The early church gradually developed rituals; baptism was one. Because there was a lot of backsliding, they started instruction periods. People could come into the church only after two years of instruction. During those two years they were admitted only to the Word service. At the end of the Word service they were excused, and the community of the faithful then celebrated their community in the Eucharist.

Being inducted into the early church meant making a profession of faith, being baptized, being taught the "Our Father" for the first time, and then there was a laying on of hands. If a bishop happened to be present, he confirmed it by laying on his hands, and then they received the Eucharist.

Gradually through the centuries the Western church separated these rituals into separate services, but in the Eastern church they continued to keep them all together. In the early church Paul had a problem of dealing with challenges to his leadership from people who were coming into communities which he had founded. These people were mixed up in a variety of Eastern cults, drugs, and the mystery religions. People were claiming ultraspiritual experiences, and claiming authority because they had them. Paul wouldn't cater to that. He said, "I would prefer to glory in my weakness, because then God's strength and God's power is made manifest."

It is one thing to come to know Jesus and in that sense to be "saved" by our initial contact with him. But it is quite another thing to lay the foundation of the Body of Christ, which Paul felt was his responsibility. The building can be on sand as well as rock. It is a fundamental part of the message that while Jesus is the foundation, there is a building to be built. There is a Body to mature. And the Lord raises up leaders to guide that. They are his ministry gifts to the community.

Paul's leadership was being challenged by people who claimed to be super-Christians. They had special kinds of experiences, so this was supposed to mean they were leaders. There have been men all through the history of the Church who have felt they were superior to other people because they had superior experiences. If one thing is clear about gifts from God, it is that they are not given because of personal worth but for building up the Body.

Spiritual experience is not the mark of being a member of the church! The church settled this very early. It said, "Membership in the church comes by submitting to the ceremony of baptism." I don't have to claim spiritual experiences. I only have to be immersed into the death and resurrection of Christ through baptism.

What does it mean to be "born again"? It is to make an

adult decision for Christ. However, I have asked people who have not received the baptism in the Spirit and have never heard of the charismatic movement, "Have you ever experienced God?" And they say, "Oh, yes, many times after Communion I feel so close to God." I've told a lot of people at retreats, "Go out in pairs and talk to each other about what God has done in your life." They come back with faces glowing; God has worked in their lives.

Spiritual experiences alone are not enough for a Christian. The marks of the Christian are faith in Christ and, incorporation into the Body of Christ as part of his life.

There is no denying that opening up further and further to the work of the Lord in our life becomes a matter of deeper and deeper expectant faith. The Pentecostals have opened up our faith in the area of the fullness of the power of the Spirit. Paul says in Romans, "How is anybody to believe unless the Word is preached?" Since we weren't preaching this, we weren't believing it to that dimension. The Lord is constantly opening up new things to us, new areas of power, new areas of expectant faith. We are always going to be growing. But to say that because somebody hasn't reached a certain stage he isn't "in the Lord" is a mistake.

At the same time Jesus was promising his Spirit, he was also praying that we would be completely one, so united that the world would know that he was sent. He wants us to be as close to each other as he is to the Father.

The foundation of Christian life is prayer, deepening our relationship with him so we can be transformed and empowered to love each other. If we are going to love each other, we are going to call each other to repentance, to turning our whole lives over to Jesus, accepting him as our Savior, our only Lord, receiving the fullness of the Spirit so we may love one another as he did.

How did Jesus love? He laid down his life for us. Jesus loves by sharing everything he has and everything he is with us. If I am to love the way Jesus loves, I have to share with my brothers and sisters in the Body everything I am and everything I have.

Agape love means I love you not because you are attractive but because I am a lover. Agape love is not a reaction to the likableness of another person. Agape is my acting from strength I have inside myself. I am a lover because I choose to be a lover, because I choose to share everything I am and everything I have with someone else. I share in the very Spirit of God, and God is love. And because I share in that power, I can claim that power to love. That is why Jesus can command us to love our enemies.

Some teachers say, "If you can't find something nice in someone, see Christ in him." I have never seen Christ in anyone except another Christian. If you love Christ in somebody, you aren't loving them. We are commanded to love people and to love them in a real way. Christian love is a matter of choice. We have the power to love as much as Jesus does. All we have to do is claim it. Love is something God empowers me to do.

The reason why Jesus commanded us to love is because he was faithful to the tradition of the Law and the Prophets. We are called to be a people, so united that we are as close as Jesus is to the Father.

Part of the Messianic presence is that the full power of the Spirit is available to the Messianic community. We are seeing that happening today.

Let me illustrate with regard to tithing. I do not see its connection to the Christian dispensation. The Lord asks *everything*. I am called upon to share everything I am and everything I have with my brothers and sisters in the Lord. That is what it means to be submissive. It is to come together out of our aloneness and isolation into total unity. I don't have to worry about giving away everything I have because the Lord will provide in every circumstance. I give totally, as Jesus gives—that includes my time, my possessions, and my secret inwardness.

Another illustration: there are real differences between denominations. As long as we don't acknowledge them, we aren't dealing with them. We aren't really one mind and one heart yet. We must confront them. We can love each other, but that doesn't mean we are of one mind and one heart yet. I have to accept you where you are and as you are, and you have to accept me where I am and as I am.

The word *church—ecclesia—*means "a people called out." It is used primarily of the local church, which is meant to be the Body of Christ. We are not called upon in just a general way to love everybody in the world who knows Christ. We are called upon to love the people we live with, the ones at our home, the ones we meet with at church. They are the ones for whom we are called upon to lay down our lives, with whom we are to share everything we are and everything we have. We are meant to be the Messianic presence encountering the local, worshiping community, people who really know how to love, to heal, to forgive. The mature Christian community is a forgiving community.

When we have gone beyond accepting Jesus as Savior and receiving the baptism in the Spirit, and have come to some maturity, we have to decide what we are going to build on the foundation which is Jesus. We can build in precious stones, or we can build in straw and wood. The fire is going to test it. If we are content with a very loose fellowship, if we have not listened to the call to love one another as Jesus loves, if we haven't yet caught the message to the Christian community, the local church, and are not loving the people we live with, then we are building with straw; we are building on sand.

We are little grains of sand that have to be welded together by the heat of love so that we become firm and solid. That is the crucifixion of community. We have to die to our isolation, our lack of communication, our aloneness, our separateness, our fear of being ourselves with each other, our timidity, so that we can be in full unity. Only when we have begun to reach that level have we begun to mature in Christ.

4

Love and Respect at Home

James H. Moore

What is God's goal for people who are saved, active in church, who love the Lord and are filled with the Holy Spirit?

I believe this is God's desire: to bring us back home, to put into operation at home all that we have learned.

If something fails to work at home, then it really has not yet been learned. This doesn't mean that we are not Christians; it doesn't mean that we don't belong to the Lord or don't love Him. It simply means that we have not yet reached the depth of what God has for us. Our home life is the test of our spirituality.

The Scripture says we are to be one. Yet God cannot mean that we are to be identical, for he has made men and women to differ.

We have to recognize that women are different from men. It is no excuse for us to say, "I just don't understand her/him." God knows fully well that we can't totally understand each other; we are different. However, we can open up and hear and receive, and as we receive from one another, we learn to

---

James H. Moore is a Southern Baptist minister who was graduated from Louisiana Tech and New Orleans Baptist Theological Seminary. He is known for his teaching on Christian family life as well as for his song leading.

understand what the other needs out of life.

A woman needs to hear her husband say, "I love you." She has to hear it over and over.

I don't like to tell my wife I love her fifteen or twenty times a day, but it's good for me. It keeps me out of my shell. It draws me out. And it meets a deep need that God has put into her heart. All of my talk and my trying to change her won't make her any different. Since her need has been put there by God, he expects me to meet it. And he has provided grace for me to do it.

How do we enter into this relationship of oneness? Two of the most important Scriptures relating to family life are 1 Peter 3 and Ephesians 5. To avoid any slavery or bondage or wrong coming upon the woman, God begins by letting her submit. He does not say, "All right, men, take over your wives."

Wives must be in submission to their own husbands. It is much easier sometimes to listen to someone else's husband than to listen to your own. But the Bible says you are to be subject to your own husband, "that if any do not obey the word, they also may without the word be won" by the way you live (1 Peter 3:1 King James Version).

"But you just don't know my husband!" That's what many a woman says. But God is making a promise here, and it works at whatever stage of unbelief your husband is in. God has to give ladies the faith to believe it and to put it into practice. You have to operate at whatever level of faith you stand. But I can promise you that God can do some astonishing things in your husband's life if you will believe God for it.

The best example in the Bible is when Sarah was obedient to Abraham (see Genesis 20). She submitted to what Abraham wanted to do. He didn't want the responsibility of having a wife; he said, "You're a pretty nice-looking woman, and they are going to cut my head off for that. So when the king comes, I'm going to tell him you're my sister." (That wasn't exactly a lie; she was actually his half-sister.)

When the king came and saw this beautiful woman, he wanted her as one of his wives. He said, "Who is this?"

Abraham said, "This is my sister."

Sarah didn't say a word. She knew her husband wasn't telling the exact truth. He was a great man of faith, a man of God; yet he was, for all practical purposes, betraying her.

The king took Sarah home. But the Lord brought trouble to the land, and God came to the king in a dream and said, "Don't put your hand on that woman; she belongs to Abraham."

God did this because Sarah did not rebel. Instead, she believed that God would keep her. She submitted unto whatever Abraham wanted her to do, believing that God would take her out of the situation, and he did.

Women sometimes say, "But my husband demands that I do things that are immoral." I cannot in honesty tell any woman to submit to a husband who wants her to do something immoral. But I believe that ninety percent of the time a woman can submit, that God can deal with the man, and that sometimes God's dealings are quite dramatic. In general, wives should be in subjection. Put yourself under your husband, for if you rebel you will get hurt.

I am not telling you to become mealy-mouthed. But the Bible does say that if your husband is an unbeliever, he can be won without your saying a single word to him. Men are never won to God by women preaching at them. You will not nag him into the Kingdom of Heaven. God himself is going to have to draw him.

Recently a woman said to me, "I realize now that I wasn't a good wife when I first received the baptism in the Holy Spirit. I went home, got out my Bible, and tried to prove to my husband that this was the way to go. Maybe I preached a little too hard or pushed a little too much."

This drives a man away; it does not draw him at all. In fact, he begins to pick at you. He watches for you to make just one slip, and when you do he pounces right on top of it.

You ought to go home and just be a good wife. Cook the best biscuits you've ever cooked. Find what pleases him. Show him that you love him. A woman is persuaded by what is said, but a man is persuaded by what he sees. When he sees a change beginning to take place at home, he will begin to change.

In my relationship I have found that as long as my wife argues with me, I don't have time to talk with God. To get my attention away from him, I try to pick an argument with her. I prove that I'm right. But if she says, "If that's the way you believe, Jimmy, that's fine," and backs away, she knows I am going to be touched. She is backing off and saying, "Okay, Lord, get him!"

The Lord says, "Okay, Jimmy, who are you going to talk to now?" The pressure begins to build. Try it. Your husband will "behold your chaste [way of living] coupled with fear" (1 Peter 3:2).

In this way Scripture deals with what men consider to be the biggest problem: "My wife talks too much." (What does the woman say? "He won't ever talk to me!")

I am not telling wives to put the lid on and never talk. What God wants in you is a meek and quiet spirit. You have to be quiet on the inside.

Don't meet your husband at the door just to say, "Let me tell you how bad the kids were today!" Meet him with a quiet and meek spirit. You can do it if you stay in a relationship with Jesus that keeps you at peace.

I know when my wife Dotty has been with the Lord—and when she hasn't. I can walk into the house and just feel these things in the air. I know whether her spirit is quiet and whether the things she needs to talk over with me have been talked over with the Father first.

Now we move to verse 7. "Likewise, ye husbands, dwell

41

with them. . . ." *Dwell* means to take up a constant abode. Don't dwell on the golf course. Don't dwell in your fishing boat. Don't dwell at your job. Dwell with your wife. "Dwell with [her] according to knowledge." In other words, get to know her. Dwelling with her is not just coming in and flopping down to watch the baseball game or read the paper. It is taking the initiative in knowing and understanding.

How many men know what is going on in their own families? How many keep track of their children? How many know where their wives are spiritually? You cannot be a leader in your own home if you do not know what is going on!

Recently, in the Atlanta airport I noticed a book about how to be a good executive. It told of a study of New York City executives who had suffered physical or nervous breakdowns. One cause: no real family life. Their homes were hell on earth.

A counselor was hired to come in and teach these men how to get acquainted with their wives and meet their needs, even if it meant spending less time on their jobs. They realized that when things are okay at home, a man will give more to his job in one hour than he will give in three hours if he has to go home to hell every night.

". . . Giving honour unto the wife" (verse 7). How do you honor somebody? If the president of the United States were to walk into my home, and we continued doing our own thing, would we be honoring him? No. To show our honor and respect, we would come to attention. We would look at him and listen to him.

For a man to honor his wife means to look at her and listen to her. It is essential that you listen. But you must listen with your heart as well as your head. She is not trying to get facts or logic across to you. It is feeling, deep feeling, that she is expressing. Some of these feelings are right and some are not, but she is trying to get them out. That is why so many women go to psychiatrists; they can talk, and sometimes they get better because they get these feelings out. If they could talk to their husbands, there would probably be much less need for psychiatrists.

". . . Giving honour unto the wife, as unto the weaker vessel." Outwardly a man seems physically stronger than a woman. But a woman can endure much more pain, which fits her for childbirth. She is less susceptible to illness. She lives longer. A male baby is much more likely to die than a female baby.

So what does the Bible mean when it calls the wife "the weaker vessel"?

A vessel is a container, something you put something into. If the vessel is weak, it breaks if you put too much into it. I believe that what is being said is that a woman cannot hold things inside her as long as a man.

One of the most capable Bible teachers I have ever heard told me, "Jimmy, I think this is the way God made us women. We have to talk at least every three days. If we go beyond three days without really talking, confusion sets in."

Any man knows that the greatest weapon he has against his wife is just to get quiet and not talk to her anymore. There is nothing, absolutely nothing, more painful to her than that. And if she keeps everything bottled up inside her, or if you make her feel guilty about it, then it is all going to come out in some physical disease or some emotional change that is not good. It will begin to bring sickness into your family.

A woman is a weaker container; she has to talk, whereas a man goes from project to project. After he gets married, he feels he has finished the project of getting married, and now he turns to the project of making a living. He forgets about the things he did before he was married.

Because I want to submit to God, I had to learn that my life is bound up with my wife. She has what I need in order to be whole. And I have what she needs in order to be whole. As the head, I am to take the initiative to see that we both become whole. We are heirs together.

I am not telling you something I learned out of a book. I

have learned it through experiences in my own life as a Christian man. I learned most of it by failing repeatedly. I still fail. I've given up hundreds of times, but God has always rescued me and said, "Okay, Jimmy, let's try it one more time." Proverbs 24:16 says, "A just man falleth seven times, and riseth up again." Take everything a little bit at a time and try to put it into practice.

Ephesians 5:19, 20 exhorts us to speak "to yourselves in psalms and hymns and spiritual songs, singing and making melody in your heart to the Lord; giving thanks always for all things unto God and the Father in the name of our Lord Jesus Christ." Thank God for the husband you have. Thank God for the wife he gave you. You may not *feel* thankful, but don't worry about how you feel; just give thanks to the Lord. Your home may be in a difficult situation, but begin to give thanks to God that he is able to change that situation. Do it in the name of the Lord Jesus.

"Wives, submit yourselves unto your own husbands, as unto the Lord" (verse 22). If you are doing it for your husband, you are serving the Lord Jesus. If your husband likes his coffee perked, but it's so much easier to make instant, submit and make perked coffee. Say, "Lord Jesus, I thank you that I can serve you perked coffee." (Don't tell your husband that; just tell the Lord quietly.)

I have a bad habit of leaving my clothes lying around. (However, I'm learning to change!) One day God showed my wife something. She was putting my shoes where I should have put them, and God said, "Do you know who wears those shoes? Do you know where those shoes go? As you put them away, bless them. Remember that the Lord uses those shoes to carry your husband and my message wherever he goes. Just lay your hands on them and bless them. Turn that irritation into a ministry."

Even if your husband is not saved, submit as far as you

possibly can. God can use even him to bless your life if you will submit to him. God can use him to guide you, direct you, keep you. But God can never speak through your husband if you are in rebellion against him.

"The husband is the head of the wife, even as Christ is the head of the church: and he is the Saviour of the body. Therefore as the church is subject unto Christ, so let the wives be to their own husbands in every thing" (verses 23, 24).

Christ laid down his life for the Church. That is love. Love is very patient. Love is long-suffering. Love is very kind. Love is very tender.

If a godly woman wants anything, she wants you, her husband. Not your money, not your popularity. A woman of God wants you. She wants you to pay attention to her in little ways. Rather than buying her a $1,000 gift on Christmas, did you know you can come out a lot cheaper by buying her little things all the year long—and that it means a lot more to her, just because she is a woman?

And remember that when a woman says, "I love you," and "I hate you," both inside of two minutes, she is not talking about what you think she is. She has been offended. She has been hurt. And what she is saying is, "I hate what you are doing."

When a man says, "I hate," you know something is seriously, abnormally wrong. But when a woman says this, she is saying what she is feeling at that particular moment. Don't explode. Don't react. Try to understand why she is feeling this way.

Notice that the Bible never tells a woman to love her husband. In Titus it does say that they will be taught how to love, or how to put their love into practice, but there is never the command, "Wives, love your husbands." The Bible does say, "Husbands, love your wives."

I believe that as the Lord cleanses the Church of guilt, so it is the man's responsibility to cleanse his wife of guilt. If it is a false guilt, one that should not be there in the first place, he should help her by being understanding. I talked with a lady recently who had a tremendous burden for her church because it isn't teaching the gospel. (It's tough for a woman to carry a burden and be a good wife and mother at the same time.) This lady told me how she was doing everything she possibly could to try to bring her church back to the right place. It was ruining her spirit.

I said, "You know, you're really not responsible for changing that church."

"That's right. That's right!" she exclaimed. All she needed was to be relieved of the guilty feeling that she was failing to do the job. A woman doesn't need to go around trying to be a crusader all the time; all that does is push the guilt back down to where it comes out as kidney infection or tuberculosis or emotional distress or something else.

"Husbands, love your wives, even as Christ also loved the church, and gave himself for it; that he might sanctify and cleanse it with the washing of water by the word, that he might present it to himself a glorious church . . ." (verses 25-27). That is the way the man is to present his wife when he gets before the Lord. He will say, "Lord, here she is."

"No man ever yet hated his flesh; but nourisheth and cherisheth it" (verse 29). The word *cherish* means to impart warmth. A mother pulls a baby close to her to nourish it and to give it the warmth and strength from her own body. So a wife needs to be warmed up. Cherish her. Nourish her, as the Lord nourishes the Church.

Man never hates his own flesh. The last time I got off the plane and picked up my luggage, a little steel prong jabbed into my finger. It would not have been natural for me to say, "You stupid finger! All you do is get in the way all the time!"

Instead, I said, "Ow!" I washed it off and put a handkerchief on it. So you treat your wife just as you treat your own flesh.

As I mentioned earlier, the Bible never says, "Wives, love

your husbands." Because a husband's basic need is not love but respect.

A woman is like a sounding board. She is made in such a way that if a man gives his love to her, it will come back to him. If you put genuine love in her, it is just like speaking into a PA system. The love will be amplified and will come back in much greater proportion.

On the other hand, the woman must make her husband feel like a man. Don't criticize him. Don't hurt him. Don't cut him down. Don't make him feel like a little boy. Listen with an ear to understanding whatever he is trying to tell you.

Many a husband is all bottled up inside, because he tries to tell his wife what is going on at his job, and she ends up making him feel like a little boy who doesn't know how to run his business. He doesn't feel respected or honored.

A man is egotistical. His need is for this ego to be built up. So reverence your husband. If he doesn't feel like a man any where else in the world, let him know that you really believe in him. Do it by faith if you have to. Lie a little every now and then if you have to! But project your faith in your husband. Build him up. Make him feel like a man. He needs it.

You shall be one.

Part Three

The Holy Spirit Empowering

5

The Spirit in Jesus' Life: A Pattern

Thomas A. Smail

Very soon after I came into the baptism in the Holy Spirit in 1965, two external attacks made me doubt the experience. I was reading a little booklet by Kurt Koch, who has written much about the deliverance ministry, including a book on the Indonesian revival. In *The Strife of Tongues*, Koch says he has come across this gift again and again, and in his opinion only one case out of a hundred is of the Lord; ninety-nine are of the devil. That really stopped me in my tracks.

At that same time I told a prominent evangelical minister and writer in Glasgow what had happened to me. He looked at me sadly and said, "Ah, yes, another of these emotional experiences. Give it three months and it will be gone, and you'll be back where you were."

Since "back where I was" was on tranquilizers during the day and sleeping tablets at night, it wasn't a very alluring

Thomas A. Smail is general secretary of Fountain Trust in London. After receiving an honors degree in philosophy at Glasgow University and a B.D. with distinction at Edinburgh University, he did a year of postgraduate study under Karl Barth at Basel. He served several Church of Scotland parishes and then a congregation in Belfast before moving to London.

prospect. I wondered if he really thought that was the normal Christian life: sleeping tablets, tranquilizers, and going to heaven when you die?

I found the answer to both these attacks in the same place. The answer to Kurt Koch came merely by looking at what the exercise of the gift of tongues was doing in my life. It was not just giving me thrills or vague religious experiences. It was bringing me into the presence of the Lord Jesus Christ, risen and exalted in a new and direct way. I knew the devil doesn't do that.

I began laughing and saying, "Well, I must be the one out of the hundred or something, but I know that through this experience the Holy Spirit is bringing me into the presence of the Lord Jesus Christ."

I was also brought through the other challenge—that what is emotional doesn't last. That is quite true, of course. If only one's emotions are being touched, then you know it won't last. But what we are talking about isn't merely something that happens emotionally. It is Spirit touching spirit, and what Spirit does to spirit abides; it has its source in the Lord Jesus Christ.

This is my subject: the work of the Spirit in the life and ministry of Jesus. This is the basis for deciding if and how and when and what has happened to us is the genuine article. If it comes from him, if it resembles him, if it glorifies him, then we are safe; it is real. But if we get out of the sphere of Jesus, we're into the sphere of trouble.

When Luke wrote his Gospel, he planted the lines he was going to develop in the Acts of the Apostles. If you start with the book of Acts, it is like going into the middle of the big picture; you don't really understand what's been happening before.

Regarding the Holy Spirit, Luke begins the trail as far back as John the Baptist, who, by the way, Jesus described as the greatest of all the prophets (7:28). Isaiah, of course, wrote chapter on chapter, as did Jeremiah, but as far as we know, John the Baptist prophesied only two things. Yet Jesus said he was greater than all the others. Apparently his predictions were of absolute importance.

Both were about Jesus. "I baptize you with water," he said in 3:15, "but"—*one*—"he who is mightier than I is coming, the thong of whose sandals I am not worthy to untie;"—*two*—"he will baptize you with the Holy Spirit and with fire." That was the extent of John's prophesying. But these tremendous things apparently made him the greatest prophet the world has ever known.

The following section ties together his two predictions:

Now when all the people were baptized, and when Jesus also had been baptized and was praying, the heaven was opened, and the Holy Spirit descended upon him in bodily form, as a dove, and a voice came from heaven, "Thou art my beloved Son; with thee I am well pleased."

... And Jesus, full of the Holy Spirit, returned from the Jordan and was led by the Spirit for forty days in the wilderness, tempted by the devil. And he ate nothing in those days; and when they were ended, he was hungry. The devil said to him, "If you are the Son of God, command this stone to become bread." And Jesus answered him, "It is written, 'Man shall not live by bread alone.' " And the devil took him up, and showed him all the kingdoms of the world in a moment of time, and said to him, "To you I will give all this authority and their glory; for it has been delivered to me, and I give it to whom I will. If you, then, will worship me, it shall be all yours." And Jesus answered him, "It is written, 'You shall worship the Lord your God, and him only shall you serve.' " And he took him to Jerusalem, and set him on the pinnacle of the temple, and said to him, "If you are the Son of God, throw yourself down from here; for it is written, 'He will give his angels charge over you, to guard you,' and 'On their hands they will bear you up, lest you strike your foot against a stone.' " And Jesus answered him, "It is said, 'You shall not tempt the Lord your God.' " And when the devil had ended every temptation, he departed from him until an opportune time.

And Jesus returned in the power of the Spirit into Galilee, and a report concerning him went out through all the surrounding country. And he taught in their synagogues, being glorified by all.

And he came to Nazareth, where he had been brought up; and he went to the synagogue, as his custom was, on the sabbath day. And he stood up to read; and there was given to him the book of the prophet Isaiah. He opened the book and found the place where it was written, "The Spirit of the Lord is upon me, because he has anointed me to preach good news to the poor. He has sent me to proclaim release to the captives and recovering of sight to the blind, to set at liberty those who are oppressed, to proclaim the acceptable year of the Lord." And he closed the book, and gave it back to the attendant, and sat down; and the eyes of all in the synagogue were fixed on him. And he began to say to them, "Today this scripture has been fulfilled in your hearing." And all spoke well of him, and wondered at the gracious words which proceeded out of his mouth; and they said, "Is not this Joseph's son?" (Luke 3:21,22; 4:1-22 Revised Standard Version)

It was a different Jesus who came back to Nazareth. These people, who had known him because he had lived and worked there, saw the difference. They saw that he had gone away to be baptized in the Jordan and had come back a different man.

When the people at home see the difference, it really begins to count. The home folk could see the difference in Jesus, that in his baptism was an experience of the empowering of the Holy Spirit. Although he had been the Son of God from his mother's womb, although he had been born of the Spirit, yet when the call came to work, Jesus still had to be specifically empowered by the Holy Spirit.

The definitive commentary on the baptism of Jesus is in Acts 10:38. Some evangelicals have said, "Nothing really happened that day in the river Jordan," but that's not the way Peter saw it. Peter told Cornelius, "God anointed Jesus of Nazareth with the Holy Spirit and with power . . . ." That was the key to his ministry. This experience at the beginning explains all that followed—"how he went about doing good and healing all that were oppressed by the devil, for God was with him."

And we are following in his steps. We are receiving the

power he received in order to do the work he gave us. So I reply, "I've not wandered into vague mystical experience; I am walking in the steps of Jesus."

Jesus' receiving of power has three aspects. The Scripture cited first tells how the power came *into* him at the Jordan River. It tells how the power worked its way *within* him during the temptations in the wilderness. And it tells how the power came *out of* him as he began his ministry in Galilee.

All of these things must happen to us; the power must come into us, it must work its way within us, and it must come out of us. The power is given to us for our work and service.

At the moment we are baptized in the Holy Spirit, we are not yet completed; we are not ready for all that God intends us to do. I am suspicious of anybody who wants to move too quickly as soon as he receives the experience. One should hardly be baptized with the Holy Spirit on Monday and take the boat to Africa to convert the heathen on Tuesday. God has things to do in us before the real ministry in the power of his Holy Spirit begins to be revealed.

God's call always authenticates itself by its permanence. God is not in a hurry, and there are things to be done after the experience has come to us before we are ready for ministry. So it was with Jesus. And so it must be with us, particularly with young Christians. In all the enthusiasm of the new power that has come, they often run out and take on far too much far too quickly. Why? Because they didn't give the power time to work its way through them before it was ready to come out at the other end.

Where did the Holy Spirit take Jesus first of all? To the wilderness, to be tempted by the devil. He had to go there first, by himself, to get the issues straightened out before his ministry could begin.

I find this tremendously encouraging. Some of us have a marvelous honeymoon experience and think it is going to be

54

sort of "Hallelujah!" all the way to heaven. It isn't. Something goes wrong, and life stops being all glory, and we begin to wonder, "Are we wrong?" We examine our hearts and try to find sins and disobedience, or the devil, or something else to explain what went wrong.

Nothing is wrong. Soon the light begins to glow. The Holy Spirit begins to live up to his name. He begins to deal with the matter of holiness. He begins to touch the issues in our life that need to be touched before what has come from God can work its way through and can get out to minister to others. That is what happened with Jesus. He had to go into the wilderness and for forty days face up to the issues being placed before him.

I used to find these particular temptations hard to understand. I wanted to do a lot of interpreting to get them to fit the sort of temptations normal people were having. These are not the ordinary temptations that young Christians face. Average people have to face problems with sex and telling the truth and things like that.

But these are the temptations of a Spirit-filled man. They are the temptations of one on whom the power of God has come and has raised issues in his life that have never been raised before. The question Jesus had to answer was, "How am I going to use the power God has given me?" For the devil was around, not denying that power, not saying, "You haven't got it," but trying to make him use the power in wrong ways. These are also the temptations of charismatic Christians.

Of course, since we are not Jesus, it is not surprising that we fall into some of these pitfalls along the road and have to be rescued from them. Jesus didn't fall into them; here was a man for the first time since the Garden of Eden in the right place with God. Here was the last Adam, the second Adam to the rescue, and here was the same old serpent back on the trail, trying to destroy God's plans again. Even as he led Eve to use the power she had been given by God in the wrong way, so now he comes to the new Adam and tries to turn his powers into the wrong paths.

Satan's first step in the tempting of Spirit-filled men and women is to attack our assurance. An earlier voice had said, "Thou art my beloved Son." Now the enemy comes along, twice, and says "*If* you are the Son of God . . . ."

Somebody comes to me and says, "I have been speaking in tongues for three weeks now, and there is a problem I want to raise with you."

And I say, "Oh, yes, I know what it is; you think you are making it up."

And they think I am a marvelous prophet! Everybody has to go through it. The enemy has come along and said, "It is not real; you're making it up; you imagine it all." Thus he tries to lead us into the place of doubt—precisely where he tried to lead Jesus.

Satan succeeded with Eve. "Did God really say, 'You shall not eat?' " He was able to cause her to doubt the Word of God; he tried to do this with Jesus and still tries to do it with us. We will only be able to withstand Satan's lies if we are well aware that the experience that has come to us is grounded in God's promise and God's Word. Our assurance comes from the Word of God. There is no assurance from glowing all the time, because that doesn't necessarily continue. But Jesus has said, "You shall receive power . . . ." He has also said that if you ask, the Father will give the Holy Spirit, not a stone, not a scorpion. You can stand on God's Word and say, "This is not something I have made up; this is something God has promised and God has given!"

If the enemy can insert doubt, then you'll never act. You'll never begin to minister, because you won't be sure of where you stand with God. A person must have assurance to come out into the open and demand that demons depart or that a mountain be planted in the sea. You only command a mountain if you are fairly sure of where you stand with God; if Satan can attack your assurance, you'll never minister. At the heart of every revival movement in the Church has been a new emphasis on the doctrine of Christian assurance.

So the devil faces Jesus with three temptations, the same temptations which face charismatic Christians. The first is to use the power that has been given you to satisfy yourself. Command these stones to become bread, since you're very hungry. You've got lots of needs, and God has given all the power. Satisfy yourself. Use what God has given you to make your life full and rich.

We live in a rather selfish world in which a materialistic rat race goes on all about us, and it is terribly easy to transfer that over into the spiritual world. The work of the Holy Spirit comes to mean *success for me;* every need of mine is to be satisfied immediately, every illness to be immediately cured, every suffering to be immediately taken away so I end up in a kind of paradise on earth.

Jesus said, "If anyone tries to save his life, he'll lose it. If anyone tries to turn my gospel into a nice, easy passage to heaven, he'll lose it. If anyone wants to be my disciple, let him deny himself and take up his cross and follow me."

John the Baptist said, "He will baptize you with the Holy Spirit and with fire." Do you know what fire is about? Fire is about sacrifice. The Holy Spirit is a Spirit who wants to lead us away from ourselves. True, he fills us, heals us, and equips us, but we mustn't seek that for our own sake. Man does not live by bread alone; he lives by every word that proceeds out of the mouth of God. The Holy Spirit is given for new obedience, for new possibilities of service; and if that is forgotten, we are in trouble.

The second temptation that came to Jesus, and also comes to us, is to move from God's supernatural into the devil's supernatural. It is absolutely essential that we know how to differentiate the one from the other. "You shall worship the Lord your God, and him only shall you serve." In other words, you are not to be led away into something terribly attractive that looks like an easy answer but that hasn't got the name of Jesus on it. That leads to disaster.

How do we know God's supernatural from the devil's? There are three scriptural tests, and we need every one of them. The first is in 1 John 4:1,2—"Beloved, do not believe every spirit, but test the spirits to see whether they are of God; for many false prophets have gone out into the world." (Many false prophets have also gone out into the modern charismatic movement.) "By this you know the Spirit of God: every spirit which confesses that Jesus has come in the flesh is of God, and every spirit which does not confess Jesus is not of God."

I was speaking to some Methodist ministers in London, trying to make this point, and they were saying, "But look, if people get healed, what does it matter in what name they get healed? What's in a name, as long as you get healed? Spiritualists, mediums, the name of Jesus—it is all the same."

I was horrified. We cannot go one inch outside the name of Jesus!

The second test is familiar: "You will know them by their fruits" (Matthew 7:20). Some people appear to confess the name of Jesus, yet the fruits do not bear out the confession. What are the fruits of false movements? Bitterness and hate and divisiveness. So you have to test everything at both ends—at its source and where it leads.

The third test is found in 2 Timothy 1:7—"God did not give us a spirit of timidity but a spirit of power and love and self-control." The Holy Spirit is differentiated from every other kind of spirit in that he does not remove us from control; he brings us into control. He does not displace us; he cooperates with us. There are no trances, no ecstasies. Have you heard some of these astounding stories about people who had to stuff hankies in their mouths to stop themselves from speaking in tongues? Well, such tongues didn't come from the Spirit of God, because the Spirit of God never takes over in that way. He takes from nobody his self-control.

We had a terrible case in the east of England recently of some extreme American Pentecostals trying to teach people to speak in tongues. They shut them up in a room and made them say "Baby Jesus" incessantly for forty-eight hours until they were shouting so loud they could be heard all around the block. Ambulances had to take them off to the psychiatric hospital. And *we* got into trouble over this because people came and asked, "Is that what you believe?"

We said, "No, it isn't; the Holy Spirit does not need any psychological techniques, any methods, or any pennies in the slot to make his things happen. He is the Spirit who works through self-control, through the faculties of reasonable and balanced men and women." The devil can raise up all sorts of people who speak fair words and tell stories that make people flock to hear. Yet it is not the sensational story that matters; it is the name of Jesus and the results it produces.

The third temptation is to use charismatic power to try to establish spiritual superiority. "If you are the Son of God, throw yourself down [from the Temple pinnacle]." Perform some sensations and make them think that you are a lot further on than they are.

One of the complaints we hear in Britain is that we divide people into first- and second-class Christians, that we claim to have a status beyond our fellow believers who are not yet moving in the realm and power of the Holy Spirit. If we try to turn the gifts of the Spirit into a kind of silver cup to put on the mantelpiece ("See what I've got?"), we're all wrong. That's what went wrong in Corinth; that's why Paul had to rebuke that congregation. Some of them were puffed up and vying with one another to establish higher spiritual status.

In the world, people establish your status by the kind of car you drive, and it is so easy to do the same in church based on the kind of gift you have. Do you know why? Because some are not very sure of themselves. "*If* you are a child of God—you're not very sure, are you?—all right, then show them; do something flashy, and that will demonstrate it to everyone."

The question of Christian status has nothing whatever to do with the baptism in and the gifts of the Holy Spirit. The question of Christian status is settled at the Cross. We are the sons and daughters of the living God for one reason only: the Lord Jesus shed his blood for us at Calvary. It was true on the very first day that we became Christians, and it will be true at the very last day. Whatever achievements in terms of holiness or ministry success we have in the meantime do not affect our status.

Martin Luther's last words as he lay dying were, "We are beggars to the end, we are beggars to the end." If we understand this rightly, then we won't be showing off, using the gifts to put ourselves on pinnacles and pedestals. The gifts and the baptism in the Holy Spirit have to do with ministry, not with status. They have to do not with making something of ourselves but with the service we can humbly render to other people. God has given us a new competence to serve, not a new standing. From the moment we accepted Jesus, we were sons and daughters of God and will never be any more so than we are already. We may become more useful, but we'll never be more in the family than we were right from that moment.

The tiny baby born into your house can't do all the jobs father and mother can do, but let anybody doubt his status in the family, and you will fight for him. He belongs; he's as loved, as dear, as accepted, as nurtured as anybody else.

Jesus had to resolve these temptations before he could

begin his ministry. Mind you, they weren't settled forever: "When the devil had ended every temptation, he departed from him until an opportune time." Remember how Satan came back again at the very end of his ministry in those voices at the foot of the Cross: "If you are the Son of God, come down from the cross" (Matthew 27:40). There it was again: "If you are the Son . . . ." Under the pressure of suffering the tempter returns and tries to get in. He'll keep showing up, but our defense against him will be that we have already faced up to these issues, that we've had them out, and that we know exactly where we stand in regard to them.

"Jesus, full of the Holy Spirit, returned from the Jordan, and was led . . . into the wilderness," and then, forty days later, "Jesus returned in the power of the Spirit into Galilee." He was *full* right from the beginning, but now that the issues are settled, he's in the *power* of the Holy Spirit. The power has come in, it has worked through, and now it is ready to start.

"The Spirit of the Lord is upon me," he said. The ministry of Jesus was more than simple teaching; it was a ministry exercised in the power of the Spirit of God. This is what people noticed about him—not just the truth of his teaching, not just his compassion for the sinners, but the authority of the man. When he said a thing, it happened.

God's Word with God's Spirit in it always achieves what it says. This is the distinctive thing about God's Word. God said, "Let there be light," and there was light. The Spirit was in the word of Jesus so that when he spoke, things happened in the natural realm ("Who then is this, that he commands even wind and water, and they obey him?"—Luke 8:25) as well as in the supernatural realm ("What is this word? For with authority and power he commands the unclean spirits, and they come out."—Luke 4:36). We've admired this element of his ministry from afar, and only recently have we begun to realize that it is for us too. "He who believes in me will also do the works that I do; and greater works than these will he do, because I go to the Father" (John 14:12). Everything that was on for Jesus is on for us. There is nothing he did that we are not to do too.

This is what Pentecost is. It is the baptism of Jesus becoming the baptism of his people.

It was the word of a Spirit-filled man at the gate of the Temple. The disciples had the power to say, "In the name of Jesus Christ of Nazareth, walk" (Acts 3:6). This isn't something weird or strange or new. It is merely the gospel happening over again in the Church of the Lord Jesus Christ. It happens when you go his way, share his baptism, work through the issues, and are absolutely clear that what has come to you is for ministering to others. It is all in the steps of Jesus. He is the source of it, and he is the end of it.

6

Objections and Answers

Frank A. Downing

Among the objections raised by those who oppose the charismatic movement are so-called scriptural objections. These may be aimed at any of the manifestations of the Spirit or at some of our practices of prayer and praise. Most frequently, however, they specifically relate to tongues.

One can sit down with a noncharismatic and discuss rather quietly, intelligently and logically all about the manifestations of the Spirit or whether there are miracles or healings in our day.

But when the word *tongues* is mentioned, the proverbial red flag is waved before the bull. I have noted—from the housewife to the seminary professor—a change in personality, in character, in relationship and approach. Scholarship—if the person is a scholar—seems to go out the window. Prejudice rears its ugly head. The same words keep coming out: "You think you're better than I am."

Certainly we should be careful that we do not give the

Frank A. Downing has been pastor of Belvedere Baptist Church in Baltimore for more than twenty-five years. A graduate of Baltimore Friends School, Wake Forest University, and Southern Baptist Theological Seminary, he wrote his Th.D. thesis on spiritual healing.

impression that we are a superbrand of Christians because we have experienced the baptism in the Spirit. Yet even when we are careful, treading very softly and trying to be as kind and loving as we can, tongues seem to change the atmosphere. And most of the so-called scriptural objections seem to be directed toward tongues-speaking.

This is by no means an exhaustive treatment of objections, but I've taken some of the ones we hear very frequently.

The first is that the miracle of Pentecost was in the hearing and not in the speaking. We don't hear this so frequently anymore; yet I was on a seminary campus about a year and a half ago and this was brought to my attention by a professor, so it is by no means passé.

Recently I picked up a little book written by four seminary professors which set forth this view—that these unlearned Galileans did not actually speak other languages but simply spoke their Galilean dialect. The Jews of the Dispersion who had come back to the holy city of Jerusalem for this significant day in the Jewish religious calendar experienced the miracle; their ears were so changed that they heard in their own language. Because these were not first-generation refugees, they had been born in the countries to which their ancestors had dispersed. Their language was not Hebrew or Aramaic; they normally spoke the languages of their countries.

The references frequently used are found in Acts 2:6-8. "And when they heard the roaring in the sky above the house, crowds came running to see what it was all about, and were stunned to hear their own languages being spoken by the disciples.

" 'How can this be?' they exclaimed. 'For these men are all from Galilee, and yet we hear them speaking all the native languages of the lands where we were born!' " (Living Bible)

This position, however, completely disregards the fourth

verse of this chapter. "And everyone present was filled with the Holy Spirit and began speaking in languages they didn't know, for the Holy Spirit gave them this ability." Here then is the basis for our scriptural reply to this objection.

According to Thayer's *Greek Lexicon,* one of the standard works in the field, the Greek word translated *utterance* is defined as "a high, lofty, illuminated speech." This was the kind of speaking that by native ability these Galileans could not have produced. I think it is fair to say—and some commentaries do—that we could paraphrase the King James translation "gave them utterance" to say something like this: "The Holy Spirit furnished the vocabulary." There is no doubt whatever that something dramatic happened in the lives of these people so they could produce languages which they were not capable of producing in their natural minds. We simply must rule out that the miracle was in the hearing.

If it were only in the hearing, then why this emphasis on what happened to the speakers? Acts 2:4 is a specific statement about their speech. One must be rather subjective to infer that the usage of the words *heard* (verse 6) and *hear* (verses 8,11) would indicate that a miracle had taken place in the hearing. What other word would one use for receiving any kind of sound, understandable or not? One speaks of that which he has heard; it's the only way we can express ourselves. Critics are reading their prejudices into the Scripture. We must be careful on both sides of this fence that we do *not* prejudge the Scripture. That's what prejudice really is—prejudging in order to prove what we want to prove. Let us pray that the Spirit of the Lord will prevent us from taking that approach to the Scriptures, whatever our theological or doctrinal position happens to be.

The second objection is the assertion that modern tongues are unlike the tongues at Pentecost. The tongues at Pentecost were known languages through which the gospel was preached and people came to know Jesus Christ as Lord and Savior. The tongues of today, it is claimed, are like the tongues of Corinth, which are classified by the objectors as mere ecstatic, unintelligible utterances—gibberish, in other words. They base their position primarily on Acts 2:6-12.

And when they heard the roaring in the sky above the house, crowds came running to see what it was all about, and were stunned to hear their own languages being spoken by the disciples.

"How can this be?" they exclaimed. "For these men are all from Galilee, and yet we hear them speaking all the native languages of the lands where we were born! Here we are—Parthians, Medes, Elamites, men from Mesopotamia, Judea, Cappadocia, Pontus, Ausia, Phrygia, Pamphylia, Egypt, the Cyrene language areas of Libya, visitors from Rome—both Jews and Jewish converts—Cretans, and Arabians. And we all hear these men telling in our own languages about the mighty miracles of God! They stood there amazed and perplexed. "What can this mean?" they asked each other.

This is pointed out as saying that the tongues at Pentecost were intelligible languages. But that set of verses describes only one of the reactions at Pentecost. Read just one verse further: "But others in the crowd were mocking. 'They're drunk, that's all!' they said." What some heard that day was likened to the rantings of inebriates, people who had had so much to drink that they were thick-tongued and their speech was not intelligible. There were two separate and distinct reactions at Pentecost.

Peter stood up and said, "No, they're not drunk; it's only nine o'clock in the morning."

When critics look for other pretexts, they go into the fourteenth chapter of 1 Corinthians and single out a number of different verses, such as 2, 5, 6-14, 16, 23, 27, and 28. These are all statements that deal with the fact that tongues must be interpreted. Paul is writing to these Christians in Corinth

66

in the context of the *public* worship service. And he is setting forth the fact that these public tongues utterances must be interpreted. Why? Because these are speech utterances which are not understood by the listeners.

To say that these are merely ecstatic utterances is an overworked phrase. The objectors use it, and you see it in all kinds of papers and books objecting to modern-day tongues. To assert that, because something is not understood by a listener, it is therefore an unintelligible, ecstatic speech is ridiculous.

We readily agree that if a person hears only tongues, he won't know what's going on. There has to be interpretation. However, many have had individual experiences where an expression in tongues did not need interpretation: it was understood by another in his native language. Harald Bredesen tells about being on a mountaintop, having gone aside to pray. He had this glorious filling with the Spirit; he began to speak in tongues. He had to tell somebody about it. So he walked down the mountainside. An old fellow was seated on the front steps of a little cabin. He tried to tell him in English about his experience, but it came out in tongues! The old gentleman's face brightened up and he came back with a stream of the same kind of utterance. Harald just stood there. Then the old man said to him in broken English, "How is it that you speak such perfect Polish, but you do not seem to understand a word of my reply?"

I was once in a service with a lady who grew up on the Russian border. That night the tongues utterance came through me, and there was an interpretation. After the service this lady came up and said, "Pastor, I did not need the interpretation. I had the translation. You were speaking in perfect Russian."

I went to another place and addressed a group. A seminary professor with a Ph.D. in Hebrew was there, and he told them afterward, "This fellow Frank Downing is a charlatan. He pulled a fast one on you. He just addressed you in Hebrew and passed it off as being able to speak in tongues."

One of the men came to me and told me about it, and I said, "Brother, he doesn't know how I struggled to pass Hebrew in seminary! Today I can hardly repeat the Hebrew alphabet, let alone speak fluently."

The same condition exists today as in the New Testament narrative: there are languages that are known to someone in the audience, and there are other utterances that are unknown. This is precisely the combination we find on the day of Pentecost. When people insist that 1 Corinthains 14 would warn against tongues, we need to take them at last to the twenty-second verse. Tongues are not a sign for Christians; they are a sign for unbelievers. The key is the word *sign.* If you study Acts 2, you discover that tongues on the day of Pentecost were actually a sign to the unbelievers.

The third objection is that tongues cause division and are therefore not of God. Many who voice this take us to John 17:21. Jesus prayed "that they all may be one; as thou, Father, art in me, and I in Thee, that they also may be one in us: that the world may believe thou hast sent me" (King James Version). He prayed for unity, for oneness in the Body of Christ. And the blanket statement being made these days is that anything that causes division is not of God.

But when we look at the Bible, we see that God has caused division in many ways. In Genesis 6 and 7 we have the description of how God directed Noah to take his wife, their sons, sons' wives, and the animals as he described them, giving lesser numbers for the less desirable ones and greater numbers for the more desirable ones. "Take them all on the ark that I direct you to build"—and we all know the story. Significant is the fact that when they all got on the ark, the Bible says God shut the door. That was it; that was division; nobody else could get on. They were all God's people by virtue of creation, yet he divided his people.

Among the people of God in Moses' day—when they were disobedient, when they sinned and rebelled, when they brought back the report that they couldn't take the land, and all the rest of it, what did God do? Did he say, "Well, I forgive all of you; you're all my people. Come on into the promised land anyhow"? That whole generation, except for two men, God cut away; he separated, he divided. These were his people! One can rebel against God, but that doesn't mean he's not his child anymore. If you're a son, you're a son. Yet God divided; he separated.

The first thirteen verses of Matthew 25 are that familiar parable of the wise and the foolish virgins. They all are virgins; they all are invited to the wedding feast; they all have their lamps. The only distinction is that the foolish ones didn't take any oil with them. Some had the oil and others didn't. When those who didn't have it returned, they were separated and not allowed into the wedding feast.

I cannot agree with the position that if anything causes a division in the Body of Christ, it is of the devil. Historically, when Martin Luther saw that the just are saved by faith and he tacked his theses on the door, he wanted only to reform the Roman Catholic Church. But division occurred, although God was the one who had directed him. What motivated Luther was the Word of God. "For by grace are ye saved through faith; and that not of yourselves: it is the gift of God" (Ephesians 2:8). This was division; yet it was a move of God.

We need to make a distinction and say that when God moves, very frequently there are *reactions* that are not of God. It is the reaction of man that is responsible for the division.

The fourth objection, a very frequent one, is "Well, yes, I know tongues are biblical, but they are not for our day." This position is based upon 1 Corinthians 13:8-10.

All the special gifts and powers from God will some day come to an end, but love goes on forever. Someday prophecy, and speaking in unknown languages, and special knowledge—these gifts will disappear. Now we know so little, even with our special gifts, and the preaching of those most gifted is still so poor. But when we have been made perfect and complete, then the need for these inadequate special gifts will come to an end, and they will disappear (Living Bible).

The most prominent proponent of this view is Dr. Merrill Unger, who formerly taught at Dallas Theological Seminary, a fundamentalist, nondenominational seminary. He says something like this: "I have been a student of the Bible for forty-five years. I read the Greek fluently, and I know when I read the word *perfect*, the Greek word *teleion*, that it never refers to a person. Those who say that *perfect* refers to Jesus Christ are going against the fundamental principles of Greek grammar."

Dr. Unger continues in similar words that "God has revealed" to him that *perfect* refers to the canon of the Scriptures. In the first century the New Testament had not yet been collected. Letters were circulated, of course, so they needed all those miracle gifts of the Spirit, but now, says Unger, we have the perfect, complete Bible, God's final word to man, and we no longer need these gifts. That which is perfect—the Scripture—has come. The Bible is closed, and the word *perfect* means "mature" or "completed."

Charismatics are asking, "What will we do with this objection?"

First, Unger has set himself against the basic interpretation of this passage all the way back to Tertullian (A.D. 160-230) and Augustine (A.D. 354-430). We can go to other commentaries that are considered old stand-bys, such as Matthew Henry, or we can check what is considered very modern and rather liberal, *The Interpreter's Bible*. About ninety-eight percent of all the commentaries indicate that the correct interpretation is a reference truly not to a person as such, but to an event which involves a person, the Second Coming, the return of our Lord Jesus Christ. That has been the age-old interpretation almost without exception, but this dear brother has invented something new. He has come up with this because he is doing his very best to find a scriptural objection to the tongues of our time.

The word *perfect—teleion* —is a reference to the Second Coming. Therefore tongues, knowledge (not ordinary knowledge, but the divine gift of knowledge), prophecy, and any other manifestation of the Spirit will not be done away with until Jesus returns. We won't need them then, because the Scripture says, "When we see him, we shall be like him." We will have no need for these imperfect manifestations at that time. We will experience the completion of our salvation. We're enjoying the first fruits now, for we have, as Paul says, the earnest of our inheritance, the down payment. But the best is yet to come.

The fifth objection: everybody knows that tongues were a problem in a problem church. That's what all of 1 Corinthians is about, they say, and then point to the fourteenth chapter. Paul uses a whole chapter to deal with tongues and the problem it was causing in the church at Corinth.

The answer on the basis of Scripture would begin at 1 Corinthians 11, where there is a discussion of the Lord's Supper, which also was a problem. But I do not find any of these critics saying, "Let's discard the observance of the Lord's Supper." Yet, when you read about the problems Communion was causing—some gorging themselves in the sin of gluttony around the Lord's Table, getting drunk, and not discerning the Lord's Body—Paul says, "For this very reason many are sick among you, and some of you are even dying an untimely death." Paul never said to stop observing

71

it because it was a problem. He was instructing the Corinthians to observe the Lord's Supper properly. Similarly, Paul wasn't saying in 1 Corinthians 14, "Don't use tongues because they create problems." He was instructing rather to utilize them correctly. His instructions are about correct usage at a public worship service.

The sixth objection: tongues are the least of the gifts because they are mentioned last; Paul listed them in order of importance.

Howard Ervin writes, "This line of reasoning proceeds philologistically in somewhat the following manner: major premise, the gifts of the Spirit are always listed in the order of their relative importance; minor premise, tongues are mentioned last. Therefore, they are the least important." Ervin goes on to say, "There are deceptive pitfalls in the use of logic that quickly expose the fallacies in a priori assumptions which are dictated by polemics rather than by rational considerations. The truth of the syllogism does not rest in the consistency of its deductions." The logic may be consistent, but it rests in the validity of the premises from which it stems. If you don't start with the right premise, you can follow all the principles of logic and come out with the wrong conclusion. It may be formally correct but substantially wrong. If either the major or the minor premise is factually wrong, its conclusions will of necessity be wrong no matter how cogent its logic may seem. Consequently the conclusion drawn in the syllogism above can only be true if its premises are true. What are the premises? The major premise is that the gifts are listed in order of their importance; the minor premise is that it was listed last because it was least important.

Does the Apostle Paul arrange the gifts of the Spirit in order of their importance? Nowhere does he state or even imply that he lists these gifts in such order. In 1 Corinthians

12:8-10 tongues are listed next to last; in verse 28 of the same chapter they are last. But in 1 Corinthians 13:1,2 tongues are listed first, and in 1 Corinthians 13:8 tongues are second in the listing; in Ephesians 4:11 and Romans 12:6-8 tongues are omitted altogether. In addition, the order seems to be different in every case. Not only do tongues change in the order given, but all the gifts change position. Indeed, Paul does not seem to have any particular scheme of order; rather, he seems to list the gifts as they come to mind. As Ervin observes, "Even a casual reading of the schismatic arrangement of these seven lists reveals a number of omissions, transpositions, and substitutions in Paul's tabulation of these gifts of the Spirit." One also notes that in these lists Paul sometimes combines the gifts of the Spirit with ministry or administrative gifts. There is no evidence in Paul's listing that would support the premise that lesser gifts are mentioned last.

The seventh objection is that tongues are evidence of a childish mind. This is based on 1 Corinthians 13:11. "It's like this: when I was a child I spoke and thought and reasoned as a child does. But when I became a man my thoughts grew far beyond those of my childhood, and now I have put away the childish things."

Our answer is based on 1 Corinthians 14:18, "I thank God that I 'speak in tongues' privately more than any of the rest of you." Even agnostics and atheists who have read the letters of the Apostle Paul have spoken of the brilliance of this man that comes through the writing. It is true that the writing was inspired by the Spirit. But God's inspiration was not like a secretary taking dictation from a boss. It was a dynamic inspiration in which God gave the truth to the individual writers, but their personalities were involved and the mental powers which they had were put into usage so their different points of view became manifest.

We see this very plainly in the four Gospels. Matthew, with

his Jewish background and Jewish way of thought, described how Jesus Christ fulfilled all the Messianic prophecies. Luke gave a Greek point of view, a more logical presentation. In John we find a presentation that appealed to the Gentile mind; that's the reason many of us especially love his Gospel. You can recognize the personality of the writer. And this brilliant man Paul, highly educated, who studied at the feet of Gamaliel, said, "I speak in tongues more than all of you." Are we to say he had a childish mind? Utterly impossible!

Another objection: Jesus never spoke in tongues. This is based primarily on the accounts of his baptism (Matthew 3:16; Mark 1:10; Luke 3:21,22; John 1:32-34). There is no mention of any tongues. Tracing through the synoptics and the fourth Gospel there is never any mention of Jesus speaking in tongues.

In response: Jesus was of course silent on many matters, and an argument from silence is not a valid argument. However, I would tend to agree with these critics. I don't think Jesus ever spoke in tongues. The significant thing about tongues is not the projection of one's vocal apparatus. It is that it involves a vocabulary not of man's making. In speaking in tongues, the mind doesn't furnish the vocabulary; the Spirit of God does. In Acts they "spoke in other tongues as the Spirit gave them utterance," or, as I mentioned earlier, "furnished the vocabulary." This was a high, lofty, illuminated speech, not the speech of the common man.

Think of Jesus—was there a language he did not know? Whether or not Jesus spoke in tongues, he did say that *we* *would*. In Mark 16:17, Jesus clearly promised, "And those who believe shall use my authority to cast out demons, and they shall speak new languages." It matters not that Jesus may not have spoken in tongues. His statement is clear and unequivocal.

74

7

A Practical Baptism

Dr. Edward K. Atkinson

There are three Christian baptisms, and there is one which is not Christian.

The first baptism in the New Testament is the baptism of John. People came to the river Jordan and were baptized by John the Baptist. This was not a saving baptism. This was not a Christian baptism.

When Paul came to some Christian converts in Ephesus, he found they were too quiet. He wondered what was wrong. He said, "Did you receive the Holy Spirit?" and they said they didn't know anything about it. He said, "What kind of baptism did you get?"

And they said, "John's baptism for repentance."

Paul said, "Oh." He realized what was wrong, for John's baptism was not a Christian baptism. It was not for salvation.

For each of the other three baptisms there are three categories and three elements. Visualize, if you will, a table of nine squares, three rows of three squares each. The first column is the candidate. The second is the baptizer. The third is the element in which the candidate is baptized.

Edward K. Atkinson, M.D., is a practicing anesthesiologist in Greenville, Pennsylvania, who devotes a great deal of time to a teaching ministry.

The first Christian baptism is *baptism in water*. The candidate is the repentant sinner who has accepted Jesus Christ. The one who baptizes is a Christian elder. (In our denominational churches it is usually left to the minister or pastor, but scripturally speaking it is an elder.) And the element in which the candidate is baptized is water.

The second Christian baptism is *the baptism in the Holy Spirit*. The candidate is the born-again believer. The baptizer is Jesus Christ. The element with which we are baptized is the Holy Spirit.

The third of these three Christian baptisms is *the baptism in suffering*. The candidate for the baptism in suffering is the water-baptized, Spirit-filled believer. You see, the qualifications of the candidate get higher with each baptism. In the first, the candidate is a repentant sinner. In the second, he is a born-again believer. The third calls for a candidate who is a Holy Spirit-baptized believer. The baptizer is the Holy Spirit, and the element in which the candidate is baptized is suffering.

People who are newly baptized in the Holy Spirit have a wonderful time. They are bubbling with joy and peace. Things look so rosy. Then all of a sudden it seems as if the roof caves in. That pink cloud disappears. They feel as if the rug has been pulled out from under them. They get up, dust themselves off, and think, *This is unfair. What happened?*

This is what we are going to consider: *What happened? What hit me?*

Most Methodists know that John Wesley spoke about two works of sanctification. The first was salvation, where we put on the robe of righteousness as we are washed in the blood. The second is the baptism in the Holy Spirit.

Sanctification is a process. Salvation is a progressive work. It is not yet complete. We are already saved, and yet we are still being saved. Fortunately for us, God sees us as

Jesus, because our salvation is a finished work which he finished in the twinkling of an eye. Yet we are still in the process of salvation.

The sanctification which John Wesley spoke about was the baptism in the Holy Spirit. It produced miracles even in his day. As a Quaker, I've always suspected that the Quakers quaked because they were Pentecostal. It has been stated that every revival in the Church was Pentecostal until it was squelched! To prove this, however, you would have to go back to the original records, because everything has been edited out that doesn't fit in with the later doctrine that came after the squelching.

The work of sanctification can be subdivided in a number of different ways. The first is that people begin to get *victory over personal habits*. We have heard testimonies about people who were able to throw away their cigarettes or never had to have any more alcohol after they were saved. One of my friends had a remarkable conversion on his deathbed. All of his hatred just melted and flowed out of him as the Lord dealt with him in that bed. Salvation causes many people to have victory over things that formerly had mastered them.

First Thessalonians 4:2-8 says,

> You know what orders we gave you, in the name of the Lord Jesus. This is the will of God, that you should be holy: you must abstain from fornication; each one of you must learn to gain mastery over his body, to hallow and honour it, not giving way to lust like the pagans who are ignorant of God; and no man must do his brother wrong in this matter, or invade his rights, because, as we told you before with all emphasis, the Lord punishes all such offences. For God called us to holiness, not to impurity. Anyone therefore who flouts these rules is flouting, not man, but God who bestows upon you his Holy Spirit (New English Bible).

The second aspect of sanctification is *the awareness of sin*. You may have noticed in your own personal lives that as Sunday Christians you were doing all the right things but not necessarily for the right reasons. You were getting along in the church. You were pretty good people. But then you received the baptism in the Holy Spirit, and the Lord began to do a work in your life. He began to put a finger on this or that area. You began to feel uncomfortable with this, when formerly you had been able to accept it pretty well. You began to realize that your time was not being spent to the glory of Jesus. You began to see that Scripture which says, "Whatever you are doing . . . do everything in the name of the Lord Jesus . . ." (Colossians 3:17).

I had a friend who had to give up playing cards because the Holy Spirit showed her that she was almost making cards a god. With you it might be golf, or bowling, or a lot of things. You become aware that God is saying, "In *you*, that is sin."

The third category is *an awareness of Jesus Christ and the Holy Spirit as persons.* For most people Jesus is just a theory, and salvation is just an idea. When I acknowledged Jesus as my personal Savior, after a time I became aware that he had died on the Cross for me personally, and I dissolved in tears. But still I had no great, personal response to him. After the baptism in the Holy Spirit, this awareness of Jesus as a person began to grow. I began to have conversations with him, hour after hour, minute by minute. Jesus becomes very real after the baptism in the Holy Spirit.

The fourth category under the heading of sanctification is *an awareness of Satan,* a completely malevolent, real, active person. After you have become aware of Jesus as a person, you begin to realize that something else is going on. You begin to perceive a spiritual warfare that is not of flesh and blood. Satan is alive and well, and he is out to get you, and you become aware of it. This is not what the liberal theologians say; it is not just the absence of good in the world, and it is not just evil in persons. We are aware of a supernatural devil who is actively opposed to those of us who are in Christ Jesus.

The fifth category is *a desire for deliverance.* More and

more people in the Body of Christ are becoming aware that they still have a lot of problems, and this brings terrible disillusionment. You come down from that pink cloud, and you realize that some of your problems are not under your control. We begin to hear about deliverance, and even though we don't like the idea, we begin to listen to it.

The sixth category is *increasing commitment to Jesus Christ.* Many of us are becoming aware that we cannot stay where we are. If we are standing still, we are falling behind. The Holy Spirit convicts us of greater responsibility. Greater growth lies ahead of us. We may respond or not. If we are going to respond, we are to make an increasingly total commitment to go when we are called, where we are called, to do what he wants us to do, regardless of the consequences.

This will cause friction in yourself and with those around you who do not see things your way. But if you are going to continue to walk with Jesus, you cannot stand still. You must walk. You must grow. You must progress. This is one of the exciting aspects of the Christian walk: you never "arrive." You never really get there, because there is always more, something more—more growth, more responsibility, more things for which we are called. This is total commitment.

The seventh category is *changing values and standards,* both moral and spiritual. The Holy Spirit puts you through a successively finer strainer. With salvation, God takes out the biggest lumps. After the baptism in the Holy Spirit, he puts you through a finer strainer to take out the smaller lumps. You begin to see things with new eyes. You have a new set of values which become increasingly difficult as you grow in the Spirit. He continues to work in more and more areas of your life.

In the letter to the church at Laodicea, the Spirit tells them that they are lukewarm, and that he despises lukewarm things. "You say, 'How rich I am! And how well I have done! I have everything I want.' In fact, though you do not know it, you are the most pitiful wretch, poor, blind, and naked" (Revelation 3:17).

This describes our situation sometimes even after we are baptized in the Holy Spirit. Poor, meaning we do not have much character. Blind, because we do not see things God's way. Naked, because we are not very righteous. But see the correction: "I advise you to buy from me gold refined in the fire."

That is, it is a very finely tuned, pure, Christian character which makes you truly rich. These are the robes of righteousness washed in the blood. We are naked if we do not have this robe. Jesus is what God sees if we do have the robe of righteousness.

And finally, ointment for our eyes. Ointment is again a symbol of the Holy Spirit who opens our eyes to see things. We must have oil in our lamp and on our eyes.

Another grouping is *a new call to obedience*. Note 1 Peter 1:14-16—"As obedient children, do not let your characters be shaped any longer by the desires you cherished in your days of ignorance. The One who called you is holy; like him, be holy in all your behaviour, because Scripture says, 'You shall be holy, for I am holy.' " So you see the need for a changing set of values and standards.

Last but not least among the results of sanctification is *the fruit of the Spirit*. Sanctification is the pruning and tending which brings fruit: love, joy, peace, patience, kindness, goodness, fidelity, gentleness, and self-control (or self-discipline).

Fruit does not appear quickly. When we were baptized in the Spirit, most of us got love, but it was love more for Jesus than for our fellow man. Some of the other things come only after a long period of time. Patience, for example, comes slowly, and it hurts.

In the Sermon on the Mount Jesus talked about being wary of false prophets. He said, "You will recognize them by their fruits." This goes for teachers in the Holy Spirit as well. What kind of lives are they living? Are they producing fruit? Are they disciplined?

All of these eight categories fit under the topic of sanctification—an inner, continuing working of the Holy Spirit in your personal life.

The other area developed by the Spirit is the power to witness, which comes up through the will. This power primarily relates to the unsaved world.

Here I want to make a suggestion. Those who are not baptized in the Holy Spirit often say, "I have all there is. I don't need what you have. There's no need for it. I don't have to speak in tongues. I've already got the Holy Spirit."

Doctrinally speaking, they are both right and wrong. In John 20 Jesus appeared to the ten disciples who were behind locked doors because they feared the Jews. Scripture says, "He then breathed on them, saying, 'Receive the Holy Spirit!' " This was their born-again experience. This is where they accepted Jesus as their risen Lord and Savior. They received the Holy Spirit; yet Jesus later said, "You will be baptized with the Holy Spirit, and within the next few days" (Acts 1:5). He was speaking of something else. So when your friends say, "I don't need it; I've already got it," you can tell them, "Yes, but you have not been immersed, or flooded, or filled with the Holy Spirit."

When we receive the Holy Spirit, we have power. We are the instruments God uses when there is a need that should be met. We are in the Body of Christ to minister to one another. You don't have to wait to take somebody to Kathryn Kuhlman to get healed. Pray for one another. It is the Holy Spirit who heals. If we refuse to use the gifts of God, then somebody goes away in need and unblessed.

We need to pray for each other and have concern for each other and meet our needs through ministering to one another. Jesus intends that we have a full life, an abundant life, but if we are not ministering and receiving the gifts, we will not have it. The Body will be very anemic and weak. It is in the baptism in the Holy Spirit that we come into this experience.

Part Four

The Holy Spirit Guiding

8

Mouth Shut, Mind Open

Charles Hunter

I want to share with you some ways to have closer communion with God in your everyday life. If we let him come into us, but we stop him there, Jesus won't stay very long, because he doesn't live in a dry, thirsty land. The only way we can be fresh with flowing water is when we let it flow through us into someone else's life. This is the beautiful pattern God has set.

God gave everything in heaven and earth to Jesus Christ his Son, and as soon as Jesus got it he gave it to us. And if, as soon as we get it, we give it to someone else, it winds up glorifying God in Christ Jesus. It starts a swift circulation of fresh water as he really does live his life in us and through us in the power of God's Holy Spirit.

Remember that Jesus comes into your heart to bring life. You're born again—you're a new creature—when Jesus is living in your heart in reality. The ideal way to let the water flow is to lead others to Jesus.

Charles Hunter's work as a certified public accountant in Houston has given way in recent years to an evangelistic ministry with his wife Frances. Together, the two have written four books; they are members of the Church of God (Anderson, Indiana).

Jesus was always talking to God, and the amazing thing is that God was always talking back. That's my subject—how to keep your mouth shut and your mind open. Keeping your mouth shut allows God to pour facts into your mind. But how does this work when you're in a certified public accounting office carrying responsibility for $100,000 of somebody else's money—that is, whether they save it or lose it in a tax matter? How do you let the Holy Spirit's power come in to instruct you on how to make that decision?

When you're talking to somebody on the phone—perhaps a neighbor—how do you allow God to speak to *you* so that you can in turn speak to that neighbor correctly?

You can be sure only by faith. You simply ask God, and you accept what he says, if you really believe in him. Then when he speaks to you, open your mouth and speak it out in faith.

The Bible is the Word of God. If you ask God for an answer to something and he gives it to you, that's also the Word of God. Whenever God speaks, that's his Word. But whenever he says something, it will always be in agreement with the Bible. Frances and I have learned to step out in faith on what he tells us. And we've found that God really does a lot of talking.

He could come out of the woodwork and say, "Charles, I want you to go hold a miracle service." But in the New Testament God speaks through the power of the Holy Spirit. So if we simply learn to listen, if we want to hear him more than anything else, and we want to obey him, to do what he says—we'll find that we actually have a two-way communication system with God.

If you're baptized in the Holy Spirit, his answers will come to you in your own way—perhaps not the same way as in my life, but you will hear from God in your daily walk.

About four years ago, after a lifetime of church service, of working my heart out, teaching Sunday School, and engaging in all aspects of church work—I met Jesus in a real, personal way, and I just turned everything over to him. I said, "God, take all of my life and make me what you want me to be." I merely "turned loose" of Charles Hunter, and I waited for God to speak.

Four months later he spoke: "Go into my Word; listen to no man; let me tell you what I want you to know." I knew he meant for me to listen to him; he was going to do the talking. He didn't say, "You ask me what you'd like to know, and I'll tell you." No. He was instructing me.

I wasn't asking him, "Is this okay, God?" I simply started letting him teach me as I dug into the Word of God. I was saying, "God, let your Holy Spirit reveal these truths to me."

How did God speak these eighteen words to me? They came to me very clearly, and yet with all of my heart I can't remember exactly how they were spoken. It wasn't an audible voice, it wasn't a thought; it simply came to me so firmly that I would stake my life that it came directly from God.

I obeyed him, and he transformed my life as I spent two thousand hours in the first year searching the Word of God. It wasn't studied systematically. I merely prayed as I read. "You talk to me, God. You tell me what you want me to know." He began dealing with my attitudes, my time, my interests in life; he took away every desire and instilled in me a desire to obey him only, and gave me an assurance that I could trust him to guide my life into any area he might want me to go. He never told me step by step what the next day's work was. But each day he told me just a little. I merely obeyed that instruction moment by moment.

It wasn't very long before he spoke again: "Cut down to half-time in your accounting practice."

That seemed a silly thing for God to do. My wife had just died, and I had all the time in the world. My natural tendency was to work longer hours. My clients loved me and I loved them. I loved to work. But God said to cut down to half-time. So strong was that message that I called a meeting with my partners and staff.

"I have no idea what he wants with that time," I told them, "but I feel that God is telling us to bring in some young men and train them to be partners. He wants to let them have the business so they can take my place as the executive part of this firm." I expected an argument, but the Holy Spirit took care of it. They were surprisingly agreeable.

The next thing God told me fit very naturally into my years of accounting practice. I had always tried to be honest with my clients, so I would tell them if I couldn't get to their work. I didn't procrastinate and say, "I'll try to do it tomorrow." If I couldn't get to it the second day, I'd say, "There are some things I must do. Could you wait for two days, and then I'll come." And when I made the appointment I always kept it.

God said, "Do the thing that's right with your clients."

So I'd go to an atheist millionaire and say, "God has told me to cut down to half-time in my part of the practice. He also said to bring in some young men—the best the accounting market can supply—and these young men will be doing most of your work. I'll be there to guide them and help them make any difficult decisions."

Do you know what the Holy Spirit did? He went to about three or four hundred executives around Houston—business owners, doctors, lawyers, Christians, non-Christians, wealthy people, poor people, sick people—as I saw them one by one over a period of eight months. I found that the Holy Spirit had beat me to every one of them. Not one of all that clientele resisted in any way, although many had previously told me, "We like your work, so don't try to send anyone else around as a substitute." Yet they accepted it without argument. I was obeying God. Within my heart I didn't care what happened as long as I could trust God to tell me what to do and then go do it.

When my wife Jean was dying with cancer, God sent me into the Bible to learn one thing: how to get myself into the position in which I can release myself totally to God. I searched in the Bible for a thousand hours in the first six months of that period. Then God brought a person by the name of Genevieve Parkhurst from Woodward, Oklahoma, into my life. She had said, "Pray, and I'll be in touch," and she had sent me a book on healing the whole person.

I started reading that book during the day. At twenty minutes till eight that evening my wife was so weak that her voice was barely above a whisper. She was so sick that the doctors had already told me to expect the end to come anytime within the next week. But that didn't bother me at all, because I was prepared for whatever God wanted to do—even if it took her life. I knew God had a plan for my life and her life, and I knew it would be all right.

When Miss Parkhurst called that night, she prayed with me and then with my wife. When she hung up, Jean's voice came back strong, and she went to sleep. Even with sedation she hadn't slept for twenty-four hours. She went soundly to sleep for the next twelve hours. So I sat down to continue reading the book.

I vividly remember sitting in the hospital room with nobody except a sleeping wife, and a voice spoke to me out loud. It simply said, "Jean is healed."

For a moment I was startled. God spoke in a unique manner because he was putting a call on my life. He was taking somebody out of my life whom I loved very much and moving me into a whole different world. He was taking Jean to be with him.

Later that night I lay down on the hospital cot. I wasn't asleep yet, and I began to see, directly above me, my own body lying eighteen inches over me. I began to feel vibrations which became stronger. I saw myself rising a little higher and then I saw Genevieve Parkhurst with her hands behind my back. She was lifting me up even as she had prayed, "I'm going to lift you into the presence and light of Jesus Christ for the healing of Jean." Jean was ready for God's call in her life, and so God was making me ready too. He was healing me spiritually as I was lifted to where Genevieve's hands could no longer reach. I just kept going up, ever more rapidly, and the vibrations got stronger and stronger until it seemed that my whole being was shaken with vibrations. I was taken to some place beyond a point I had ever seen or imagined, and there I was bathed in a brilliant light and just held there for a moment before I started back down. As I descended, the vibrations lessened until finally I was back in myself again.

I had read where Paul was lifted into the third heaven. I don't know about my case, but in some way I was lifted up into the very light and presence of Jesus Christ and bathed in it. God was really dealing with me that night. It was the most exciting night of my life to that date. (Some nights since then have been more exciting. Praise God! I know why he's going to give me a new body when I get to heaven; this one is going to explode one of these days here on earth because of the excitement Jesus Christ brings as he lives his life in and through me in the power of God's Holy Spirit. When Jesus lays my hands on somebody's head and all of a sudden that person is healed! or a big arthritic lump disappears—yes, some nights have been almost too exciting to handle.)

About two or three o'clock I looked over at the cancer which was drying everything in Jean. She lay there trying to get the tiniest little bit of moisture on her lips, but there was no moisture there. I said, "God, would you drop some moisture in her mouth?"

And God replied. He simply said, "Charles, let me do this my way." They were silent words but emphatically spoken. So I lay there a few more minutes and observed something else from which Jean was suffering. I asked God again. Soon that silent voice was there once more: "Charles, let me do this my way." I lay there a few more minutes, and again I prayed for something else. His voice came back exactly the same way: "Charles, let me do this my way."

I said, "Yes, Lord. You do everything for the rest of my life your way; I'll never try to do anything my way again. I'm simply going to ask you to tell me what to do. I'll do anything you tell me to do, and I don't care what it is." My human heart wanted Jean to be healed. But for the first time I completely released her and said, "Yes, Lord. If you want to take her to heaven, that's great with me. If you want to leave her, that's great with me. Anything. Do it your way, and I'll simply obey."

God spoke three times in three different ways in one night. How could I ever doubt my Lord Jesus as he speaks by the power of the Holy Spirit?

The other night in our home prayer meeting—which has grown so large that we had to move to a motel—a man with long gray whiskers came up. I asked, "Do you know Jesus as your Savior and Lord?"

He replied, "Yes, I do."

I asked, "Have you received the baptism in the Holy Spirit?"

He answered "Yes"—and over backwards he went under the power of God. Nobody touched him except Jesus. That's another way in which God may speak to you.

The other day a very belligerent young man came up to Frances. His mother had accepted Jesus. He had his hands in his pockets, his long greasy hair was hanging down, and he said, "I don't know why I have to come up here."

Frances said, "I know. You haven't accepted Jesus as your Savior." He answered very politely, "No, ma'am."

She said, "Pray this prayer."

So Danny started saying, after Frances, "Lord Jesus, forgive my sins; come into my heart, and make me the man you want me to be." When he had said that, he added defiantly, "Nobody's going to knock me down under the power. I'm not going to fall."

Frances simply said, "Jesus, touch him." And down he went.

People get up and say that God talked to them there on the floor. One young fellow said recently while lying on the floor, "I didn't feel anything." So he tried to get up. But God said, "I've got something I want to talk to you about." And he couldn't get up until God got through talking to him.

This first young man was so belligerent that he went down with his hands in his pockets. They were still in his pockets when he hit the floor. The next day we got a phone call from his mother. "My son talked with me for an hour this morning," she reported, "and he said, 'When I went down, I felt a great power which lifted me up and laid me down. While I was there, a big cloud came over me and parted. I didn't see anything, but a voice came down, and it said, "Danny, I want you to listen to me and obey me." ' I looked in the Bible where it said a big cloud came over one day and a voice spoke and said, 'This is my beloved Son.' "

God speaks to people in many ways. One night in a service in New Mexico, Frances had taught something about cigarettes, and people were being delivered of them. One man sitting about two-thirds of the way back said disgustedly, "Aw, bull! I'm getting out of here!" So he stepped out of his seat into the aisle. But the power of God hit him so hard he fell back in his seat. He just couldn't get up no matter how much he tried. Then God said to him, "You go out to the car and get that carton of cigarettes. I'll let you get up as soon as you tell me you're going to do it."

In a few minutes we saw a man coming up to us with a carton of cigarettes. He said, "God said I had to do this before he'd let me off the floor." Praise God! He was delivered from cigarettes.

God speaks to us also by giving us his wisdom. In 1 Samuel

10, Samuel was anointing Saul as king over Israel, and he
told him that when he met a band of prophets, he too would
begin to prophesy. "And you will feel and act like a different
person. From that time on your decisions should be based on
whatever seems best under the circumstances, for the Lord
will guide you" (verses 6,7 Living Bible). It was only when
Saul sinned and disobeyed God that he started to make
mistakes.

In James 1:5 God is again speaking about how he guides us
in making decisions. "If you want to know what God wants
you to do, ask him, and he will gladly tell you." God has the
answers, and he wants to tell us. We need only to learn how to
listen and understand what God is saying. The only way to
understand what God is saying is to *want* to understand and
want to obey it. If we want to hear, he is always ready to give
a bountiful supply of wisdom to all who ask him.

Have you ever been confused about whether God is telling
you to do this or that? Do you ever have to make a decision in
your business one way or the other? How do you get those
answers? How do you know?

Frances and I have come to release ourselves completely as
God has done so many miracles in our lives that we reached
the point of not really caring what God tells us to do. He
doesn't always give the guidance plainly, because he wants
us to seek him and his ways are not our ways, so he'll cause us
to go into the Bible and search for the truth. Sometimes he'll
cause us to ponder and pray for days.

I can give you an example from my business. One day I
needed an answer to a very complex, very costly situation. I
could either save hundreds of thousands of dollars for my
client in taxes or I could cost him that much. It was a heavy
responsibility.

Even with my training, my knowledge of the tax laws, and
my library, it was extremely difficult. The gobbledygook of
government language becomes so complicated; it will say,
"As mentioned in chapter two of abc," and then go back to a

thousand different references and add "except for when . . ." the laws just twirl your mind around until you become so confused you don't know where to go.

So in searching the laws I have learned simply to say, "God, you know the answer, and you know how to take my mind with all the training I've had and all the knowledge I have and take me from there into the answer to this problem." Sometimes I've had to look in tax laws for two days, searching and searching. I've said, "God, let me know when I get there."

Just as he told Saul, "Your decisions should be based on whatever seems best under the circumstances," so I daily expect the Lord to guide me. I merely use my natural ways, and when I come to the answer, I know within my heart that this *is* the answer, and I can be certain of it. But I search and search until I have that assurance in my heart.

My client first called me about two o'clock in the afternoon and said, "I'm getting ready to go into a two-million-dollar land deal with one of my friends here. He's already checked out this tax structure with his lawyers and C.P.A. Now he wants to come in and get your approval, because I'm not going to do anything unless you say it's okay." I had taught him that he doesn't dare change his tax structure without clearing with me, because when he does he gets in deep water, and sometimes I can't get him out of it. I always tell him to come to me first.

I suddenly realized this must be a complicated problem that I knew nothing about. They got there about four o'clock. The man with my client was a Jewish lawyer who began to speak rapidly even as he entered my office.

I said, "Wait a minute! Take it a little more slowly."

He answered, "With your experience, you should be able to understand it. I don't want to waste any money. I'll tell it real fast because it's all approved anyway. All you have to do is say okay to your client."

But I don't work that way. I operate under the Holy Spirit's power, and he won't be rushed. However, this Jewish attorney did slow down a bit, and for fifteen minutes he outlined the complicated structure of a two-million-dollar investment. His client's tax structure was one picture and my client's another. They had a proposed sale in the future, which presented another tax structure. It was very, very complex.

Now I normally spend two or three days researching all the angles in order to be certain that my client is protected. It could mean a loss of many thousands of dollars if I make a mistake. But I didn't have time. So I called on *my* Jewish lawyer—Jesus. All the time this attorney was talking fast, I was listening and praying.

"Tomorrow morning we meet," he continued, "to give an answer to the people with whom we're dealing, and we need your answer now."

As he was talking I was praying. You *can* listen with your ears and talk to Jesus too. You don't have to put it in fancy words; just throw it up there in a ball and Jesus will grab it. He knows all about it anyhow, because he knows your heart before you pray. So this time I said, "Father, you're going to have to give me a quick answer right now so I can give it back to them."

So after fifteen minutes of one of the most complicated tax structures I'd ever seen, I began to speak. I was absolutely astounded with what came out of my mouth for the next ten minutes. A tax structure flowed from me that I couldn't believe. God was reaching back fifteen years ago to something I'd read or heard; he was digging into what I had read the day before; and he was taking what I had just heard, and was putting all those things into my mind. They were pouring out of my mouth beautifully laid out.

When I finished, that lawyer looked at me and wondered aloud, "Why didn't my tax people think of that?"

You can depend on Jesus to speak the words you need. Satan is the author of confusion, and he will do everything he can to confuse you. So accept the full instructions of James and trust God totally.

> If you want to know what God wants you to do, ask him, and he will gladly tell you, for he is always ready to give a bountiful supply of wisdom to all who ask him; he will not resent it. But when you ask him, be sure that you really expect him to tell you, for a doubtful mind will be as unsettled as a wave of the sea that is driven and tossed by the wind; and every decision you then make will be uncertain, as you turn first this way, and then that. If you don't ask with faith, don't expect the Lord to give you any solid answer (James 1:5-8).

9

The Answer Book

Frances Gardner Hunter

Perhaps because I was so old when I became a Christian, I had to make up for lost time. My problem for the first forty-nine years of my life was simply that I was a great sinner! But when I met Jesus, it turned me inside out. It turned me right side up.

I do not believe that a Christian has to have a "down" period. Many people might disagree with me, but my own personal experience is that I live on top of a mountain all the time. This doesn't mean I don't have problems. I probably have more problems since I became a Christian—but I have the answer!

On that beautiful day it took me just one split second to walk from this world into eternal life. Eternal life begins on that day when you accept Jesus Christ with your heart, mind, body, and spirit—when you believe that Jesus is who he says he is and that he will do what he said he will do.

God opened the windows of heaven for me on that glorious day. I have never been the same. I saw what heaven is all

Frances Gardner Hunter, formerly the owner of a Miami printing firm, married Charles Hunter in 1970. She is the author of several popular books and is in constant evangelistic ministry with her husband.

about. I have never looked back. I have not wanted any part
of the world since then. I think that is why I stay on the
mountaintop.

People say to me, "How do you do it? Weren't you just born
that way? Aren't you just an enthusiastic, effervescent
person?"

Maybe that is part of my make-up, but it is of greater
importance, I think, to understand the little rules you have to
follow. These will help you to lead an exciting Christian life
all the time.

The day I accepted Jesus, God put into my heart the most
tremendous hunger and thirsting for his Word. I had a Bible
that I was so proud of. It was given to me in 1924, and I had
never read it. I wanted to take care of it. I never read it
because I thought it might get all messed up if I opened it.

Somebody said to me, "Do you know there are over seven
thousand promises in God's holy Word?"

"There are?" I said. "God, let me live long enough to claim
every one of them!"

I then began to read the Bible. (How are you going to collect
on God's promises unless you know what they are?) I became
a fanatic about reading God's holy Word. I used to stay up
until five o'clock in the morning just devouring it.

Eat God's Word. Read it and think about it, and grow
strong in the Lord. That is exactly what happened to me.

I asked the young pastor of the church where I found
Christ to get me one of the newer Bibles so I could understand
a little better what God's Word was saying. He bought me a
Revised Standard. I will never forget what he did when he
gave it to me. He didn't just hand it to me. He held onto it a
minute as he said, "Frances, don't you dare open this Bible
without asking God's Holy Spirit to reveal it to you."

Until you ask God's Holy Spirit to reveal the truth to you,
the Bible is not more than printed words on a piece of paper.
Only when the Holy Spirit quickens it to your heart does it
become the living Word of God.

Before I open God's holy Word, I first ask the Holy Spirit to reveal the truth to me. I pray, "God, what do you have for me today?" Then God's holy Word comes alive.

My Bible is messy. It is underlined in blue, pink, purple, green, and yellow. These are my personal love letters from God. Whenever God speaks to me, I write all over my Bible just exactly what he says at that moment.

The best place to go when you are spiritually "down" is God's holy Word. Really read it. The Scriptures will lift you and build you up and put you on top again.

I underline once if it's good. If it's really "heavy," as the young people say, I underline all over the place!

Don't worry about marking up your Bible. When it gets too messy, go out and buy a new one. You may have to buy a new Bible every year, because if you have matured during the year, God's holy Word is going to speak to you anew and afresh. We tend to get hung up on the verses we have underlined, so start all over from scratch every year. But keep your Bibles, because it's fun to go back and look over them again.

I use colored pens for different purposes. As God reveals something to me, I become excited about it, so I underline everything about that subject throughout the Bible in one color. Then if I want to look over something I can just go through and pick out all the passages marked in that color. Right now I'm using yellow on all the praise portions of the Bible. It is easier for me to look for the yellow than to memorize exactly where things are.

I will never forget the day I first read the *wow!* chapter in the Bible. Let me show you exactly what it said to me and why it turned me on, and why I wrote "Wow!" beside it.

It is the third chapter of Ephesians, starting with the seventeenth verse, and its parallel Scripture, Colossians 1:27. It tells how "Christ will be more and more at home in your hearts" (Living Bible). Here is the secret of Christianity living within you; it says, "Christ in you, the hope of glory!"

Sometimes we sing songs such as "Take My Hand, Precious Lord; Lead Me On," but the secret is that Christ is *in* you, and that is the hope of glory.

Feel your heart right now. Feel that heartbeat? Are you aware of the fact that it is the heartbeat of Jesus in you? That ought to turn you on! Some people fail to realize that Jesus Christ is living his life in you and through you. This is what makes life so exciting. He lives within you as you trust in him.

"May your roots go down deep into the soil of God's marvelous love; and may you be able to feel and understand, as all God's children should, how long, how wide, how deep, and how high his love really is; and to experience this love for yourselves, though it is so great that you will never see the end of it or fully know or understand it." Listen to this promise of God: "You will be filled up with God himself." You will be filled up with God *himself,* the God who made the universe.

The day I read that I said, "God, who am I? Who am I to be filled up with you?"

"Nobody," he said. "But I promised it."

And God does not lie.

"Frances, some day you will be filled up to the top with me," God said that day. That really turned me on. So right alongside that verse in Ephesians I wrote, "Wow!" because that is exactly how I felt.

I often wonder if, when we get to heaven, God will ask, "Did you read my love letters? Have you read them all? Have you read the Old Testament?"

Some of you may have read the book *My Love Affair with Charles* about how I met my beloved husband. I'm so glad the Lord sent me a fanatic just like me! Praise the Lord! Charles and I never had a date with each other. We met when I was on a speaking tour in Houston. I never saw him again until he came to Miami, where I lived, to claim me as his bride. In the meantime Charles wrote letters. This is how we fell in love with each other. We wrote each other about the miracle that God was doing in our lives.

Now let me ask you a question. When those letters came in that beautiful handwriting from Houston, Texas, do you think I threw them into a corner and did not read them? Do you think I said, "One of these days I'll get some time and read them"? No! When the mailman brought them, I tore them open and I read them and read them again—four, five, six, seven, and ten times.

This is exactly what we should do with God's love letter. We ought never to put this off. God's love letter should take first place in our lives.

Just after I became a Christian, I was so in love with Jesus and so grateful for what he had done in my life that I just had to get into his holy Word and read it all the time. One morning I was at the office early, and instead of doing my work I turned to God's Word. (I owned the company, so it was all right.) God somehow directed me to look in Galatians. When I first became a Christian, I just could not wait to get down to the part that really turned me on. I heard a sermon during that period about getting off the milk and onto meat. I always thought that the first few verses were the milky ones, where Paul used to give all those flowery greetings to all the brothers and sisters and neighbors. On this day, as I was reading Galatians I went *zoom* all the way down to where I thought the good stuff was.

It would have been so easy that morning to miss the voice of God. He whispered so softly, "Go back." I didn't want to go back, but I listened to God that day.

"All right, Lord," I said, and I read quickly as I could down to the meat again.

God said softly once again, "Go back."

I did not understand, but I went back and read it more slowly this time. Nothing! I said, "God, I didn't know Paul. He died quite a few years before I was born. I don't understand."

It was beautiful what God said to me then. Again it was so soft I could have passed it by. He said, "I'm talking to *you.*"

What a difference!

I looked around to be sure nobody could see what I was doing. I scratched out "Paul," and I wrote "Frances" very lightly. I thought I could erase it in case it might be a sacrilege. All of a sudden in that exciting moment I realized that God had inspired the Bible to be written for me. For me! This book was God's personal love letter to me.

I had fun that day. Do you know what I did? I went all through the Bible and crossed off "James," "Paul," "John," and "Peter." God was not talking to those fellows back then; he was talking to me!

In some of the chapters I read he got a little nasty, but I thought they must be true. (Read Corinthians and see what he tells you there when you put in your name.) God told me I was a sinner, and I kept telling him I wasn't, and he kept stepping all over my toes. Finally I gave in and said, "Okay, I'm a sinner."

I cannot think of a better way for God to speak to us about our faults than to make his holy Word personal.

Let me read you a little verse from "First Frances," the sixth chapter, the eleventh verse. (Look at my Bible sometime. I scratched out Brother Timothy's name.) As originally written, it says, "Oh, Timothy, you are God's man. Run from all these evil things and work instead at what is right and good, learning to trust him and love others, and to be patient and gentle. Fight on for God. Hold tightly to the eternal life which God has given you, and which you have confessed with such a ringing confession before many witnesses."

This did not mean very much to me, because, once again, Timothy happened to be one of those who had died before I was born. But on this beautiful day when I discovered that this was a personal love letter, I scratched out Brother Timothy's name and wrote in mine.

Now my Bible says, "Oh, Frances, you are God's woman." God is talking to me. He is telling me to be patient and gentle and to fight on. He is telling me to hold on to the eternal life God has given to me. See how different that is? When you put in your own name, it immediately gets your attention.

One verse that means more to many people than any other is John 3:16. When I was a little kid, I used to be able to recite it very fast. I got a gold star on that old Bible because I could say it so fast, but it didn't mean a thing!

Today when I open my Bible to John 3:16, it speaks to me. It says, "For God so loved Frances Hunter that he gave his only begotten Son, that if she believes on him, she shall not perish but shall have everlasting life."

Keep your Bibles in a handy place. You ought to have a Bible in every room in your house, beside every telephone. When people find out you can give them the Word of God when they call, you will be amazed at what happens to your telephone calls.

We have been having so much fun since the book *The Two Sides of a Coin* came out. We have been ministering the baptism in the Holy Spirit over the telephone. A lady called from Alaska the other day. She said, "I've never been able to receive the baptism."

"Honey," I said, "this is your day!" Before that conversation was three minutes old, she was praying in the Spirit. Jesus had baptized her in the Holy Spirit. Hallelujah!

That happens daily. Do you know why? People know that when they call, the Word of God is right beside our telephone. While we are away, my secretary answers the phone and does the same thing.

I have a "thing" about Christians who smoke. I think it kind of ruins your witness. How can you say, "Jesus is all I need," and have a cigarette hanging out of your mouth?

People call me every day and say, "I hear you curse cigarettes so people can't smoke again, and they vomit if they try."

I say, "You're right!" And I quote them a little verse of

Scripture that says, "Do you not know that you are God's temple and that God's Spirit dwells in you? If any one destroys God's temple, God will destroy him" (I Corinthians 3:16, 17). God said it, and I believe it.

I can be so firm on cigarette smoking because I smoked for thirty-five years. I smoked five packages of cigarettes a day. And then I met Jesus. Oh, boy, do I have money to give to the churches now! I'm no longer a slave to some little thing that didn't make me look very feminine anyway.

Put a Bible everywhere in your house. As a matter of fact, I recommend that you put a Bible in your bathroom. Charles and I have stayed in many homes throughout the nation, and we have a favorite little piece of "scripture" which goes, "By their bathroom literature ye shall know them!" You have no idea what we have found in the bathrooms of pastors' homes.

One time when I was speaking in Oklahoma, a pastor who heard this suggestion said, "A Bible in the bathroom!" He thought it was sacrilegious.

After we had been there a week, he thought maybe there was something to the idea. He went home and put a little tiny pocket Testament in the bathroom drawer so nobody would see it. I saw him about six months later, and he said, "You know, Frances, you were right. I've read the Bible more in the last six months than I ever have."

My son Tom was twenty-one when his mother found Christ. Mothers sort of lose their influence over their kids by that age. Tom had been raised in a non-Christian home. As a matter of fact, I was the one who bought him his first cigarettes. I gave him his first drink.

When I met Jesus, the more I fell in love with him the more Tom ran in the other direction. I'll never forget the time he said, "Mother, you're no fun anymore. You don't tell dirty jokes, you don't swear, you don't dance, you don't smoke, and you don't drink. All you do is go to church, go to church, go to church!"

I never compromised for Tom. For three years he did not

even call me mother because I had become such a "religious fanatic" in his eyes. The Bible says, "Thou shalt have no other gods before me." Not even the god of your children.

My daughter became a Christian exactly one week after her mother did. She saw what happened to me, and she decided she wanted the same thing. So we have never had a problem with Joan.

If you can imagine all the things that young people are doing today and multiply that by ten, you know what Tom has done. I love Tom despite what I say about him. I love him, but I am going to be honest with you, because I believe that in my honesty there may be some answers for some of you.

With great love I dedicated my book *Hot Line to Heaven* to Tom. It goes something like this: "There are those who hear the gospel of Jesus Christ and accept readily, but then there is the rebel who fights every inch of the way. Such is my son, Tom."

Things got bad for Tom. He and his wife decided to kill each other. They loved each other, and they couldn't live without each other, but they could not get along, so they were literally planning to kill each other.

They were not even speaking to each other when they began to call us in Houston every night from Miami just to complain about each other—each knowing that the other one was listening on the other line.

I could say only one thing. Every night they would tell me their problems, and I would say, "Jesus Christ is the only answer. Your marriage will never work until you get right with God." After that I could not say another word.

I would hang up and say, "Charles, I'm really worried about myself. That's all I can say. I can't even tell her to get the garbage out of the living room so he doesn't fall over it when he walks in the house at night. I can't even tell him to be sweet and kind to her and not so nasty and mean and hateful. I can't think of another thing to say except like a little parrot, 'Jesus Christ is the only answer. Your marriage will never work until you get right with God.' Then they get mad and hang up on me because that's all I can say."

Praise God I couldn't say more!

Last year we went to Abilene, Texas, to speak at a Full Gospel Business Men's regional convention. George Otis was to be there too. George is the man the Lord sent to have breakfast in our home, and if you have read *The Two Sides of a Coin,* you know what the Lord left behind. The Lord used him to minister the baptism in the Holy Spirit in our house.

Now watch how beautifully God did this!

He allowed our daughter to be with us on this trip. Joan doesn't often travel with us now that she is in college.

A very interesting thing happened on the plane to Abilene. The three of us were reading the book of Proverbs together. It is not a book that we read very often. When we reached chapter ten, I became convinced that the Lord had written Proverbs just for Tom. I realized that something special was happening. Here is the tenth chapter, first verse: "Happy is the man with a level-headed son; sad the mother of a rebel."

Remember the book dedication? There is a rebel who fights every inch of the way, and "sad the mother of a rebel."

Right next to it in hot pink I wrote, "Tom." Then I added in the margin, "Except for Jesus."

I would be in a mental institution today had it not been for the day I said, "Lord, here's that kid of mine. I did a messy job of raising him. I give him to you and make him your problem. He belongs to you. He's not my problem anymore." I quit trying to play God.

I prayed that God would make my kid miserable. I thanked God every time they called. I prayed that God would make him and his wife so miserable that they would be so far down that there would be no place to go but up.

We read on, and all of a sudden we came to the eleventh chapter, verse twenty-one. "You can be very sure," it says, "that the evil man will not go unpunished forever."

That day, twenty thousand feet high in an airplane, I

believe I saw the eternal destiny of my son. I saw my beloved six-foot, four-inch son burning in hell.

I'm not one of those sweet mothers who say, "Well, he's really a nice boy." His being a "nice boy" has nothing to do with it. It is whether he has been born again that counts. I knew that if Jesus Christ were to come or my son were to be killed at that moment, he would spend all of eternity in hell. There was nothing I could about it. Nothing.

At that moment my heart broke—until I read God's promise that followed next: "And you can also be very sure that God will rescue the children of the godly."

I just sat there with my eyes closed, turned my head up, and said, "God, what right do I have to be called godly? What is there about my life that could be called godly?"

Only one thing makes anyone godly. It's being born again. If you are a child of God, you have a right to be called godly.

I wrote in red ink in the margin, "Jesus, save Tom."

We had fasted that week for President Nixon and the members of his cabinet. We fasted for Tom too. Every time we would pray for all the officers we would also pray, "Jesus, save Tom."

Tom had quit his job a few weeks before. He said he did not like the printing business. He felt he didn't have to get his hands dirty to work. He asked us to send him $500. Praise God, we didn't. I found out later he wanted it for a down payment on a Cadillac! I said to him, "Honey, who is going to feed your kids?"

"I'm not worried about that," he said. "But I'm not going to get my hands dirty."

With this in mind, imagine my surprise when we read Proverbs 12:9, "It is better to get your hands dirty—and eat, than to be too proud to work—and starve." Guess whose name I put next to that?

Some day I am going to show Tom all these verses of Scripture with his name beside them.

On we read to the thirteenth chapter, verse two, which says, "The good man wins his case by careful argument; the evil-minded only wants to fight." Tom has been a fighter from the word *go*. What did God inspire me to write in that margin? "Tom (B.C.)," that is, Before Christ.

The fifteenth chapter, verse nineteen, was the next to hit me. "A lazy fellow has trouble all through life." Do you know what I call a lazy fellow? Somebody who does have enough sense to pick up the Cross of Jesus Christ and follow him! I wrote "Tom (B.C.)" again.

After that it says, "The good man's path is easy!"

Isn't that the truth! The Christian path is easy. You have all the same problems and temptations, but you have the answer!

Right then, in all of my Bibles something new began to appear. I began writing, "Tom (A.C.)"—After Christ. I stood on the promise of God that he will rescue the children of the godly.

In Abilene the next morning we had breakfast with George Otis. We were just bubbling over, telling him things that had happened since we had received the baptism in the Holy Spirit.

After a minute, George disappeared. Without my realizing it, someone had come and called him out.

An hour and a half later George came back and sat down beside me. He didn't say a word, because we were listening to a speaker. He flashed me a piece of paper with my son's Miami telephone number on it.

I nearly fell off my chair. I remembered the conversation we had had with Tom's wife just before leaving Houston. Tom had left her, and she had taken a job in a bar to make a living for herself and her children. She had told us that one night while she was working at the bar Tom had stolen the bed and television set. She had sounded so desperate as she asked, "What do I do?"

107

"Praise God," I had said.

"For what?" she asked.

"Because you don't have a bed to sleep on, and God's holy Word says to give thanks in all things," I answered. "He didn't say you have to mean it; he just said to give thanks in all things."

I think it was the hardest thing she ever did. She said, "Thank you, Lord, for the fact that I don't have a bed to sleep on, and I don't even have a carpet on the floor, so I'll have to sleep on the concrete floor."

My heart was racing. Satan was really jabbing at me, filling me with a thousand fears for my son and his wife.

I leaned across the table and said, "George, what happened? What's wrong? Did they call you, or did you call them?"

George said, "It's okay. I called them. And calm down. Nothing's wrong."

Then he gave me the most wonderful news I ever got in my whole life. He said, "Nothing's the matter. Tom and his wife have just accepted Jesus Christ."

Hallelujah!

And as soon as my son joined the Royal Family of God, the little word *mother* came right back into his vocabulary.

Amen!

Part Five

The Holy Spirit Evangelizing

10

Light in the Darkness

Larry Tomczak

"Would someone be kind enough to tell me what the word *evangelism* means?"

The priests and nuns I was addressing were dead silent.

"Would anybody like to take a guess? Maybe you could just paraphrase a definition—anyone?"

Not even the bishop who was present lifted a hand.

"Does anyone have any idea what this word means?"

We Roman Catholics aren't the only people unsure about the idea. The word *evangelism* comes from the Greek word *euangelion*, which comes from *eu*, meaning "good," and *angelos*, meaning "angel" or "messenger." An evangelist is a proclaimer of good news, a bearer of good tidings.

Every one of us is called to evangelism. It is a fact of Scripture. We may not like to think of it this way, but every one of us has been commissioned by Jesus Christ to go into all the world and preach the gospel, the good news. To preach means to advocate earnestly or publicly proclaim the good

Larry Tomczak met Christ personally while student body president at Cleveland State University (he was also the first student member of the university's board of trustees). He became a lay Catholic evangelist in July 1972; his home is now in Washington, D.C. His story is told in his book Clap Your Hands.

news of Jesus Christ, that every man and woman who walks this earth may have eternal life as a free gift by trusting and abiding in Jesus Christ. Romans 10:13 (Revised Standard Version) says, "Every one who calls upon the name of the Lord will be saved."

But let's not stop there. The next couple of lines say, "But how are men to call upon him in whom they have not believed? . . . And how are they to hear without a preacher? And how can men preach unless they are sent?" Then it says, "As it is written, 'How beautiful are the feet of those who preach good news!' " (verses 14, 15).

Young people have come to me crying, "Larry, I can read the Bible, I can pray, I can put posters up for Jesus rallies, I can do almost anything, but I can't witness at school. It's hard!"

Most people have misconceptions of what evangelism is about. But if we work at it, we can literally take the worry out of witnessing and lift the burden so that we can go out and proclaim this good news to everybody.

Until I came to know Jesus Christ as my Lord and Savior, I was in spiritual darkness. Satan, as the Scripture says, had a veil in front of my eyes. The Bible says in 2 Corinthians 4:4, "The god of this world has blinded the minds of the unbelievers, to keep them from seeing the light of the gospel of the glory of Christ."

But God has made provision, as we Christians know, for dealing with the darkness. He sent light into this world, and the light is Jesus Christ. In John 9:5 Jesus said, "As long as I am in the world, I am the light of the world."

But as you know, Jesus has left this world for a while. He has gone to prepare a place for us, and he is going to return. In the meantime, somebody else is going to have to be the light of the world, and you can guess who. In Matthew 5:14 Jesus said, "*You* are the light of the world." You and I are representing Christ; Jesus Christ wants to relive his life through every one of us. We represent the light to this world.

111

LARRY TOMCZAK

I never realized the significance of this until I went to Hawaii for a convention of the Full Gospel Business Men's Fellowship. Lawrence Welk and his troupe happened to appear at our hotel to film five TV programs and I happened to meet him. I gave him a tract and told him about Jesus. He too is Catholic, but he didn't understand what I meant about making a decision for Christ. He said, "I go to church."

I said, "Yes, I know, but have you ever personally accepted Christ?" He didn't know what I meant, just as I hadn't at one time.

Later, I went out on the beach one evening about eleven o'clock. I was all alone. Behind the hotel were the bandstands from the Lawrence Welk Show. I walked out on the platform and stood exactly where he stands. I just thought, *Wouldn't it be wonderful if Lawrence Welk came to know Christ personally and began to witness for Christ openly and publicly on TV?* I pictured him telling all the world about Jesus Christ between songs. He could reach 20-30 million people every time.

My mind was on Lawrence Welk and all the things he could do, when all of a sudden Jesus spoke in my heart. I heard the words, "Larry, *you* are the light of the world." I began to realize what I was doing. I was thinking how other people could witness, when Christ has called *me* to be the light of this world.

He has called *all* of us. He said further, "Let your light so shine before men, that they may see your good works and give glory to your Father who is in heaven" (Matthew 5:16).

Satan has distorted these words and confused Christians throughout the history of the Church. At least a thousand times in my Christian life I've heard—and I used to say myself—"Oh, I don't believe in talking about religion. People know where I stand. I'll be a witness for Christ by my conduct." That's a trick of the devil. Millions of people say the same thing, and none of them are fulfilling the order of Jesus Christ.

What is God's light to man? It is twofold: Jesus and the Word. Jesus the light is gone for a while, but he left his Word with us. His Word is like a spotlight. It illuminates man; it tells you who you are, where you came from, and where you're going.

Now if God's light is his Word, it might very easily be extended to say that *our light* is *our* word. So when Jesus says, "Let your light shine before men," what he's saying is simply, "Let your word shine out of your good works and show the whole world who is responsible for them." To paraphrase: "Let your word shine before men onto these good works so people will see who is responsible for the good works. Then they'll give credit to your Father who is in heaven."

A wonderful Christian woman in Maryland recently told me , "I don't think you have to go out and tell people about Jesus Christ. I let my light shine by my station in life. For seventeen years I've worked in a mental hospital as a volunteer; I've never gotten one cent for it. By my very presence in that hospital as a volunteer I'm letting my light shine."

I tried my best—in love—to show her that she was mistaken. For seventeen years she has never told anybody in that hospital about Jesus Christ. She's done the good works, but she's not shining the light on the good works by telling who is responsible for them. So who is getting the credit? For seventeen years people have been saying, "Oh, what a wonderful woman that Mrs. Smith is! She's such a dedicated volunteer. Hail Mrs. Smith!"

Visualize yourself dying of cancer. The doctor comes into the room, looks all around, and walks out the door. Somebody stops him and asks, "Aren't you a doctor? What about that person in there?"

And he says, "Sure, I'm a doctor. Everyone knows it; they can see my medical bag; obviously I'm a doctor."

A doctor who tries to practice medicine without opening

his bag is the same as a Christian who never opens his mouth about Jesus. A witness must be a good work and a good word back-to-back. They are inseparable. If you and I witness to everybody we can, but don't show them love, then we are robbing the gospel of its power. If on the other hand, we love everybody but don't witness for Christ, we're robbing people of the source of that love.

I was walking down the street one day and was confronted by none other than the happy Children of God. I can't pass any judgment on them; all I know is that they witnessed to me without giving me any love. I stopped to talk with one young man holding a Bible. Quickly about twelve of them surrounded me. They were quoting Scripture and telling me about Jesus, but there was no love coming from them. They were criticizing my clothes. They pointed to the cross I was wearing and said, "That's a graven image." They said, "God is calling you to come with us right now. If you don't, you're disobeying the Word of God."

Finally I couldn't take them anymore, so I just brushed them aside and walked on. If I had been an unbeliever, I would have wanted nothing to do with Christianity after that.

On the other hand: let's say Mr. and Mrs. Jones are trying to lead me to Christ. They invite me over for dinner one night. They pick me up at my home; they love me and cater to me. Mr. Jones says, "Larry, I understand you're a little short on money," and he gives me ten dollars. They are compassionate and kind. They drive me home at the end of the evening, having been the most loving people in the whole world.

Of course, it is obvious that I respect them. They gave me love. But they never said anything about Christ. I walk away from their home and tell people, "Oh, the Joneses are a wonderful couple!" The heavenly Father gets none of the glory.

Witness without love robs the gospel of its power. Love without witness robs people of the source of love.

In the spring of 1973 I was walking down a street in Washington, D.C., about two blocks from the White House. A woman was standing in the middle of the street crying. Cars were honking at her. I walked over to this woman and said, "Ma'am?"

She said, "Get away! Let me alone!" She continued crying.

I got my arm around her and somehow slid her over onto the sidewalk. She tried to push me away. "Leave me alone!" "Stop it! I want to die! There's nothing to live for!"

I thought to myself, *Maybe she's taken some pills. Maybe she's trying to commit suicide.* So within four minutes I tried to give her the gospel. She listened even though she was crying and shaking her head. I quoted Romans 10:9. I told her, "Eternal life is a free gift. I may never see you again. I don't know what has happened to you, but would you right now accept Jesus Christ as your Lord and Savior and receive the free gift of eternal life?"

I was getting anxious, because I thought she could drop in my arms any minute. But that woman bowed her head and prayed along with me for Jesus Christ to come into her life and be her Savior.

When she lifted her head, she was still crying, I walked with her down the street. We talked for one half-hour. She told how her husband and children had left her, she'd been on drink, and her life was a mess. She was also an epileptic, and suddenly I became uneasy, because this woman stopped and began going into some funny contortions. Her eyes rolled back, her eyelids were fluttering, and she was shaking all over. I was scared. But before I had time to doubt, I laid my hand upon her and said, "I claim healing in the name of Jesus Christ!"

Suddenly she expelled some short gasps and said, "What happened?"

115

I too said, "What happened?" When I got my senses, I realized that I hadn't had time to doubt. And I began to explain to her what had happened, that Christ was dwelling in her life. He had healed her, and he was now ministering to her and was going to do wondrous things in her life. We talked for another hour, went into a restaurant, and had coffee. She repeated at least twenty times during the course of our conversation, "I just can't believe that somebody would stop; I just can't believe somebody would stop for me."

This is no credit for me; she knew that the love she felt was credited to Jesus Christ and my Father in heaven, because I shone my light on it through my word. I don't know where the woman is today. I gave her some literature and talked further with her. But I know that love is a powerful thing; it has a great impact upon people. If all of us would just be free and let this love flow out from us, we would see how quickly people would come into the Kingdom of God.

A man said to me once, "Larry, none of us has been called to His Majesty's Secret Service." Jesus Christ has given us a commission to be his ambassadors, and we are to proclaim the good news to everyone.

Specifically, how do we let our love flow? The classic Scripture which illustrates this is the Gospel of John, chapter 4.

This passage is more meaningful to me as a result of my recent trip to the Holy Land. I went to Jacob's well, near the city of Samaria. We walked down some steps to the well, enclosed now by a small chapel. The well is still in operation. They lowered the bucket into the water, and we tasted it as we sat on the edge of the well just as Jesus did.

The day Jesus was there, he demonstrated five principles for communicating the good news. (I was once a salesman, and I remember the five laws of selling. It seems as if they have been extracted from the Scriptures!)

The first principle, in verse 7, is *attention*. He established a common interest with this woman, a bridge for communication. He could have gone up and said, "Lady, you know who I am? I'm the Son of God." He didn't do that. First he saw the necessity of gaining her attention. He referred to something in which she was interested—obviously, water. When he asked for a drink, she was able to provide it.

As witnesses, we want to gain a person's attention, or in other words, establish a common interest. We want to build a bridge of communication. We don't go grabbing people by the lapel and asking, "Are you saved, brother?" Most people are running from God already, and to confront them with a statement like that is no way to gain their attention.

Proverbs 16:21 says, "Pleasant speech increases persuasiveness." I talked with a priest on the plane to Jerusalem. He had been expelled from China in 1954 after working there more than thirty years and was now going to Taiwan. I asked him, "How did you go about approaching a community in China when you first went there? What was the first thing you did?"

He answered, "Well, obviously the first thing you have to do is befriend the people. Once we established a relationship, they began to trust us, and then when someone in the community died, they came to us. That was an opportunity for us to show friendship in the realm of spiritual matters."

A smile attracts people's attention. Jesus said to be of good cheer. The Bible says, "Rejoice in the Lord always" (Philippians 4:4). Proverbs says, "A glad heart makes a cheerful countenance." A heart that is abundantly full of Jesus Christ and his love will indeed make a cheerful countenance. We shouldn't restrain it. As someone said, a smile increases our face value.

We must also be good listeners. If we refuse to discover the context in which someone lives, we are refusing to discover the person himself—his values, his beliefs, his experiences, what he's made of. Proverbs 18:2 says, "A fool takes no pleasure in understanding, but only in expressing his opinion." Proverbs 18:13 tells us, "If one gives answer before he hears, it is his folly and shame." If you show a sincere interest in something the other person is interested in, he opens up like a blossom. That's what Jesus did at the well.

"The Samaritan woman said to him, 'How is it that you, a Jew, ask a drink of me, a woman of Samaria?' . . . Jesus answered her, 'If you knew the gift of God, and who it is that is saying to you, "Give me a drink," you would have asked him, and he would have given you living water' " (John 4:9,10).

The key word to the second principle is *gift*. Jesus aroused her interest when he began to talk about the gift of God. *Now what is this gift?* she wondered.

We are to be like fishermen. Jesus said, "Follow me, and I will make you fishers of men" (Matthew 4:19). Thus we throw out the bait—perhaps a comment like, "You know, I had an experience that changed my life," or, "Well, I used to feel the same way until two years ago something happened to me that literally revolutionized my entire life-style." *What is it?* they wonder.

In verses 13-15 Jesus used his third principle: " 'Every one who drinks of this water will thirst again, but whoever drinks of the water that I shall give him will never thirst; the water that I shall give him will become in him a spring of water welling up to eternal life.' The woman said to him, 'Sir, give me this water, that I may not thirst, nor come here to draw.' "

The principle is summed up in the word *desire*. Jesus was trying to elicit a desire in this woman so she would earnestly seek what he had to give. And she responded intensely.

I met a young Moslem waiter in a Jerusalem hotel whose name was Athon. He waited on our table for five days. We were as friendly to him as Christians could be. Many of us shared our faith with the young fellow. We talked to him about Christ. We let him know where we stood, and he knew about the love because he could feel it and experience it in our lives. And he also knew it was Christ who was responsible for this.

At the end of the week, we had the privilege of seeing Athon come to know Christ personally and accept him as Lord and Savior. Then we asked Athon why he wanted to accept Christ. He said, "I want to be like you people." Through our lives he developed a thirst for what we had, and he discovered who could quench that thirst.

Jesus demonstrated the fourth principle in verses 16-19. " 'Go, call your husband, and come here.' The woman answered him, 'I have no husband.' Jesus said to her, 'You are right in saying, "I have no husband"; for you have had five husbands, and he whom you now have is not your husband; this you said truly.' The woman said to him, 'Sir, I perceive that you are a prophet.' "

The fourth principle that Jesus teaches here is a *conviction of need*. Conviction—convincing—is the fourth law of selling. What Jesus had to do was to expose her sin in order to awaken a sense of personal guilt. He had to convince her that she needed what he had.

We can't come out and condemn people for sins, but we are able to use Scripture to awaken in people the sense of guilt and of need. "All have sinned and fall short of the glory of God" (Romans 3:23). For more than a year after I accepted Christ, I tried to share with my dad that it is absolutely necessary to accept Jesus Christ. But each time I would ask him, "Dad, if you were to die tonight, where will you spend eternity?" my dad's response was always, "Well, I've led a good life and I've never hurt anybody and I've been faithful in providing for my family and I've helped out in the bazaars at church and I give contributions . . . ."

It's not always easy to help a person understand that he has a need. But if we share Scripture in love with people,

119

pointing out the truth that all have sinned, and that the wages of sin is death, then we can let the Holy Spirit do the convincing.

The next thing the woman did was to change the subject (verses 20-25). This is a trick of Satan, a smokescreen he puts up.

But Jesus refused to be sidetracked. "The woman said to him, 'I know that the Messiah is coming (he who is called Christ); when he comes, he will show us all things.' Jesus said to her, 'I who speak to you am he' " (verses 25, 26).

The fifth law of selling is something we call *the close*, or closing the deal. Jesus brought this discussion to a close by direct confrontation, making this woman realize her personal responsibility to make a decision. Each one of us is called to bring people into confrontation. If we have carried them this far and they are hungry, then we must proclaim the Word of God very simply, that if they will confess with their mouth that Jesus Christ is Lord and believe in their heart that the Father raised him from the dead, they will be saved (see Romans 10:9). Another helpful passage in closing, in leading them to make this commitment to Christ, is Revelation 3:20—"Behold, I stand at the door and knock; if any one hears my voice and opens the door, I will come in to him." We share with them that the door represents their life, and an individual must open up this door.

In addition we should stress urgency; the Word of God says, "Now is the acceptable time; . . . now is the day of salvation" (2 Corinthians 6:2). "Today, when you hear his voice, do not harden your hearts as in the rebellion" (Hebrews 3:7, 8).

With the power of the Holy Spirit, something will happen if we've gone through this method of Christ's—gaining attention, arousing interest, creating a desire for what we have, bringing them to a sense of conviction of their need of Christ, and then bringing it to a close. I believe in following the method of Jesus. If we do, we'll see people coming into the Kingdom of God. We'll be turned off occasionally, but I want to make sure that when I reach heaven I have many, many friends there who will say, "Thank you, Larry, for sharing Jesus with me."

11

Jonah Learns a Lesson

Michael Esses

The book of Jonah is hard to understand. Some defend it as truth, others call it fiction. This, of course, causes confusion among readers.

The book teaches that Jonah's adventure was for the purpose of learning a lesson—a lesson for himself, for Israel, and for all of mankind.

The lesson involves much more than simply the need for repentance. God does accept repentance, but if that were all, chapter four of the book of Jonah would be irrelevant. The message also is more than that heathen are God's creatures and are worthy of pardon.

Jonah was reluctant to deliver God's message of salvation to the people of Nineveh. He felt that if he had to deliver such a message, it was going to cost him his faith in the living God. This is the way Jonah saw it: how dare the Lord pick a Hebrew and send him into the enemy camp to preach a

---

Michael Esses is the son and grandson of Orthodox Jewish rabbis. He had completed rabbinical training when he had a personal encounter with Jesus the Messiah. Fluent in Hebrew, Aramaic, Arabic, and Chaldean, he is the author of two books and now ministers at Melodyland Christian Center in Anaheim, California.

message of salvation? Jonah begrudged the fact that God was going to grant salvation to the people of Nineveh if they accepted his message and repented. It is this grudging attitude which is so superbly rebuked throughout the entire book.

So the essential teaching of the book of Jonah is that nobody, Hebrew or otherwise, should ever be denied or begrudged God's love, God's care, and God's forgiveness.

Jonah the son of Amittai is mentioned in 2 Kings 14:25 during the reign of Jeroboam II. This puts him in the first half of the eighth century before Christ. We are told that Jeroboam "restored Israel's border from the entrance of Hamath as far as the sea of Arabah, according to the word of the Lord, the God of Israel, which he spoke by his servant Jonah, the son of Amittai, the prophet from Gath-hepher." Thus we know Jonah's exact time and place in history.

"The word of the Lord came unto Jonah, the son of Amittai, saying, 'Arise, get yourself up from where you are sitting. Arise and go to Nineveh and proclaim against it, for their wickedness has come up before me.' " So Jonah heads for Tarshish, a seaport in Spain. He goes there to flee from the presence of the Lord. He is not fleeing from the Lord, but from the *presence* of the Lord. He knows he cannot escape from the Lord, but he does not want to hear the Lord's voice. He goes to escape the Shekinah of God, the Holy Spirit.

But the Lord wants Jonah in his perfect will, so he hurls a great wind into the sea. There is a mighty tempest, and the ship is about to break into pieces.

Many modern historians have stated that this is just an allegory, that the story of Jonah never really happened. But I praise God for Jesus Christ who verifies and confirms. Jesus said, "As Jonah was in the belly of the fish three days and three nights, so shall the Son of man be" (Matthew 12:40). Jesus confirmed that the book of Jonah is true. He confirmed that every word of God in the Bible is true.

The Lord sends a great wind, and the ship is about to be broken. The mariners are afraid. Each cries out to his own pagan god. To lighten the ship, they throw their wares overboard. Where is Jonah? He is totally unconcerned. He is down in the hold, fast asleep. He is escaping from the presence of the Lord, from the voice of the Holy Spirit saying, "Go to Nineveh."

The ship's master wakens Jonah and says, "Pray to your God. Perhaps your God is the true God. Our gods aren't answering us. You call upon your God, and perhaps we will not perish."

And then they say, everyone to himself, "Come, let us cast lots that we may know for whose cause this evil is upon us." So they cast lots, and the lot falls upon Jonah. And they say, "Tell us, we pray you, for whose cause this evil is upon us? What is your occupation? Where do you come from? What is your country? And of what people are you?"

And he says to them, "I am a Hebrew, and I fear the Lord."

"So why are you escaping if you fear the Lord? What kind of an affirmation of faith is this?"

Now the men are exceedingly afraid, for they know he has fled from the presence of the Lord. They are afraid of the living, true God. Then they say unto him, "What shall we do unto you that the sea may be calm?"

And Jonah says, "Toss me into the sea!"

These men have been touched by the witness that he has given them, so they refuse to throw him in.

Notice the power in witnessing even to heathen: they now cry unto the Lord and say, "We beseech thee, O Lord, we beseech thee, let us not perish for this man's life, and lay not upon us innocent blood! Cause us to do it another way, we beseech thee!" They are calling upon the living God.

But the storm grows worse, and finally the sailors capitulate. They toss Jonah into the sea, and a miracle happens. Immediately the sea becomes calm. The men fear the Lord exceedingly. They offer a sacrifice unto the Lord, and they make a vow. They say, "We are going to give a pledge, a tithe, and an offering, and we are going to believe in the living God." They have turned from idolatry and have come to know the living God.

(Hebrew oral tradition tells us that on the day of creation God created Leviathan, a certain fish, for the sole purpose of swallowing Jonah!)

Jonah is in the belly of the fish for three days and three nights. While he is there, he prays. "I called out of my affliction unto the Lord, and he answered me. Out of the belly of hell cried I, and you heard my voice. I cried unto you, Lord, and I know you have already heard my voice, and the answer to my cry has already been answered."

He says, "The weeds were wrapped around my head. I went down to the bottoms of the mountains; the earth with her bars closed upon me forever. There was no way out except you, Lord, the source of all life. I had to look up, and I did look up, and I did call upon you, Lord, and I know you heard my voice. You have brought up my life from the pit of hell, O Lord, my God. When my soul fainted within me, when I had nothing left, by your Holy Spirit, you caused me to remember you, Lord. I remembered the Lord, and my prayer came in unto you, into your holy Temple.

"They that regard lying vanities forsake their own mercy." In other words, they who get hooked on anything else but the Lord Jesus Christ forsake their own mercy.

He continues praising God and says, "But I will sacrifice unto thee with the voice of thanksgiving. I'm going to thank you, Lord, for the circumstances I find myself in. I'm going to thank you for the seaweed wrapped around my neck. I'm going to thank you, Lord, that I am down at the bottom of the sea. With a voice of thanksgiving I am going to praise you!"

And as soon as Jonah finishes praising the Lord, the fish

throws him up on the dry land.

Then the voice of the Lord comes again saying, "Arise, get up. Go to Nineveh."

Jonah obeys. He isn't going to run away this time. He knows now that he has nowhere to run. No matter where he goes, the Holy Spirit is going to come upon him and give him the same message.

Jonah goes to Nineveh, an exceeding great city. He enters the city and proclaims the message the Lord has given him. "You have forty days in which to repent. If you listen, and if you believe God's Word, and if you do repent, deliverance is at hand."

The people of Nineveh believe the message of God. They repent with sincere hearts. They turn away from evil. Nineveh is saved.

But Jonah isn't happy. He has a new problem. He says, "I knew all along that you were going to save those heathen, so why did you have to put me through all this? Why didn't you do it all yourself? Why did you have to use me?"

Jonah pouts. He continues, "Kill me. Go ahead. Take my life from me, God. I want to die. You saved those heathen. You saved the enemies of Israel. I don't want to live any longer. Kill me. If you don't do it, I'm going to do it myself."

The Lord responds, "Jonah, are you really so angry with me?"

Yes. Jonah is really that angry. He goes out to the east of Nineveh, builds himself a booth, and sits there, waiting to see what is going to happen to the city. Maybe he thinks the Lord will change his mind.

It's hot out there. Jonah could die of sunstroke. So the Lord makes a gourd to grow up over Jonah to shade him from the sun. And Jonah is glad for the shade.

But during the night the Lord prepares a worm, and the worm eats the gourd, and the gourd dies.

Then the Lord makes the east wind blow, and the sun is scalding hot. Jonah faints. But before he faints he says,

"Well, it's better to die than to live anyway."

God says to him, "Jonah, are you really angry with me? First you were angry because I saved Nineveh. Now you're angry because I killed the gourd. Are you really angry with me, Jonah?"

Jonah retorts, "Yes, I'm angry with you! I want to die! I can't figure a God like you—all the love and mercy and kindness and forgiveness!"

And the Lord, so patient, says to Jonah, "You had pity on that little gourd, and you hadn't done a thing to make it grow. You didn't plant it. You didn't water it. Should I not have pity on Nineveh? There are a hundred twenty thousand persons in that city who never knew right from wrong before I sent you to them. Should *they* not have an opportunity to respond to my voice?"

And finally Jonah understands. He gets the message. Salvation is not to be denied to anyone. God is no respecter of persons.

Praise the Lord!

Part Six

The Holy Spirit Healing and Delivering

12

Divine Healing: Fighting the Good Fight of Faith

A. Herbert Mjorud

Jesus declared, "I came that they may have life, and have it abundantly" (John 10:10 Revised Standard Version). It is not an abundant life when you have a body so full of disease and pain that you can hardly think straight, let alone pray. Psalm 107:17-20 says that some were sick due to their sinful ways, but the Lord sent his Word and healed them.

Proverbs 3:1-8 begins with an exhortation to keep the Word of God. One should bind God's commandments about the neck and write them on the tablets of the heart, trusting the Lord and acknowledging him in all things. He closes with this promise, "It will be healing to your flesh and refreshment to your bones."

And in Proverbs 4:20-22, we have a similar exhortation about listening to the Lord. "My son, be attentive to my words; incline your ear to my sayings .... For they are life to him who finds them, and healing to all his flesh." Physical life and spiritual health result from the Word of God.

A. Herbert Mjorud, long-time American Lutheran pastor and evangelist, was a lawyer before entering the ministry. A native of Alaska, he now speaks to audiences all over the world, often on the subject of healing.

"But for you who fear my name the sun of righteousness shall rise, with healing in its wings" (Malachi 4:2). Jesus Christ is the Sun of Righteousness, according to the last book of the Old Testament.

In the last book of the New Testament, Revelation 22:1, 2 says, "Then he showed me the river of the water of life, bright as crystal, flowing from the throne of God and of the Lamb through the middle of the street of the city; also, on either side of the river, the tree of life . . . and the leaves of the tree were for the healing of the nations."

Is it the will of God to heal? What does the Word say?

He brings the revelation to us, and he says, "Now *you* act; *you* respond." But if we say, "Lord, heal me if it be thy will," we're saying, "I don't believe what you said, Lord." It's like playing checkers. The Lord moves; he brings the revelation, and then he says, "All right, now it's your move. Your move is *faith*. You respond according to what I have directed you to do."

If we say, "Lord, if it be thy will, heal me," we're really saying, "Lord, I want you to move again." In a game of checkers, if one person won't move, the game is over. The same is true in the Kingdom of God. The Lord says, "Ask, and it will be given you; seek and you will find; knock, and it will be opened to you" (Matthew 7:7). "Whatever you ask in my name, I will do it" (John 14:13). But ask! "Whatever you ask in prayer, believe that you receive it, and you will" (Mark 11:24). "Hitherto you have asked nothing in my name; ask, and you will receive, that your joy may be full" (John 16:24).

The crisis experience is asking and then moving out in faith to claim what you asked for by the promises in the Word of God. Ask in faith, believing.

When I came into the experience of the Holy Spirit, I still had a lot of reservations about healing. But the Lord pushed me off the brink right into it. The very first place I went after I received the Holy Spirit was a home where a woman was stricken with a heart attack. The husband said, "I was just going to call the doctor and the ambulance when you knocked at the door." As soon as I came in, he ran for the phone.

I said, "Why don't we pray for your wife?" He agreed. So the pastor prayed, I prayed, and he prayed.

Then the Spirit of God said, "Now *you* go lay hands upon her and claim healing for her in the name of Jesus." I had never done that before. But the Spirit of God told me to do it, and that's exactly what I did.

The power of God fell upon her right then, and she was healed just like that. That ushered me into the healing ministry!

Thereafter I had to reexamine my theological concepts, looking again at the Word of the Lord to see what he had to say about healing. My mind had to be reoriented.

Some people think the prayer of faith is to pray incessantly, asking, pleading. I know an elderly Pentecostal man who was seeking the Holy Spirit. He came to my room, and I said, "How long have you been seeking the Holy Spirit?"

"Well," he said, "I guess it's been about forty years."

"You've prayed often for the Holy Spirit?"

"Yes, every time there's a prayer meeting I'm always there and praying."

"I guess you have prayed a thousand times for the Holy Spirit."

"Oh, yes, at least" was the reply.

I then said, "If you had prayed the prayer of faith the first time you prayed, you wouldn't have had to pray any longer, because the prayer of faith will release the Holy Spirit." Many, many people have prayed many, many times about many things. But when you know the will of God and you know the Word of the Lord, plan to pray once. Put your request before the Lord in a very definite and positive way. Whether in your prayer closet or at a prayer meeting, just say, "Lord, this is going to be it. I'm going to have hands laid on me; then I'm going to believe."

Now it's God's move, right?

Kenneth Hagin, who is a healer in the true sense of the word, says, "I don't pray for the sick unless I have preached three sermons on faith, because most people don't believe what the Word of God says on healing." But he himself believed as a boy seventeen years old. A congenital heart disease had paralyzed him from the waist down. His illness was terminal. He was a dying young man.

When he was converted, he began praying for healing. He prayed very, very earnestly for two years, and nothing happened until a revelation came to him from Mark 11:24. He discovered he was not praying in faith; he was "praying in hoping" . . . hoping that the Lord would heal him.

Hope is not faith. In the thirteenth chapter of 1 Corinthians, three things are mentioned: faith, love, and hope. Faith and love are two different things, and likewise, faith and hope are two different things.

Kenneth was praying, hoping he would be healed. The Lord says we are to pray and *believe* we are healed, and then it will be done. So he prayed and believed; he praised and magnified the Lord. Then a miracle happened. His heart was healed, and the paralysis left his body. When he began praising and magnifying the Lord, the Lord heard him and provided his healing. All he had to do was appropriate the promise and claim it. It didn't happen right away, but now he's a walking miracle if there ever was one. Two deadly problems in his body, which would have taken his life, were healed totally.

Many, many people seek such miracles. God performs them, sometimes even though the faith is generated by someone else. Most people want that kind of thing to happen to them. It's wonderful to have a miracle in your body while your faith is not involved. But God also deals with people for themselves. He says, "Be it done unto you as you have believed." And then people are really stuck, because they aren't believing. Even Christians are lazy when it comes to faith. The Lord wants us to learn to walk and live by faith, so that faith is the experience of our life, and we exercise it in order to grow up in every way into the Lord.

It's a marvelous thing to walk in the dark when all you've got is the Word of God, as Abraham did. For years he was given the promise, "In thee shall all the families of the earth be blessed" (Genesis 12:3 King James Version). He didn't have a son, and Sarah was already elderly.

When he was eighty-six years of age, they took the matter into their own hands to have a child from Hagar. Abraham came before the Lord and said, "Oh that Ishmael might live in thy sight!" But the Lord said, "No, but Sarah your wife shall bear you a son" (Genesis 17:18,19 RSV).

Abraham believed God. And the Bible says that this was counted for him as righteousness. He kept on believing, praising, magnifying the Lord, fully convinced that God was able to do what he said. And as he gave God the glory, his faith waxed strong. He didn't have any evidence—only the Word of God. He couldn't say, "I sure feel as if we're going to have a baby." He couldn't say, "Sarah is expecting." But he gave glory to the Lord, fully convinced that God was able to do what he said he would do. That's faith.

Sometimes we too have to walk in the dark. We have only that word to sustain us. Sometimes the Lord permits us to be tested. He puts us out in the panorama of life to see if our faith will live. Through all the testings of Satan, our own minds, and the world in which we live, he wants to find out whether or not our faith is genuine and real. How do we fight the good fight of faith? What do we do while we wait for our healing to be physically evidenced? Most people don't want to wait. I don't either. But as we wait on the Lord, he renews our strength.

So we fight the good fight of faith in the name of Jesus. We pray, "Lord, let it be done to me according to your Word. I believe that you are my Redeemer, and I know that you are my healer. I know you took my sins on the Cross, and I know you took my infirmities there also. I believe, Lord, that you were made sick that I might be made whole; I believe that through your stripes I am healed."

Are you ready to make your request before the Lord? This is what healing is all about: letting the requests be made known. If you knew no other verses than John 14:13,14 where Jesus said, "Whatever you ask in my name, I will do it"—how would you pray? You'd say, "Lord, I'm sick, and I'm asking for healing in your name. Amen."

When Mary and Martha prayed for their brother Lazarus they simply said, "Lord, he whom you love is ill" (John 11:3). The Lord certainly answered that prayer, didn't he? It was short and to the point. The Lord looks at our heart for faith.

Someone asked me, "Do you believe in the second blessing?"

And I said, "Yes, and the third and fourth and fifth, ad infinitum." Receiving and receiving . . . what a joy!

We know we can go to heaven even if we're sick. But we will never get there if our spirits haven't been made alive. So that's the main thrust: *We must be born again,* just as Jesus said.

However, many Christians live on a very low plane. They are like the the prodigal son who stayed home. You notice that I called him a prodigal son too. He was in his father's home, but he was also a prodigal, because he said, "Why didn't you do something like this for me, father?" Why don't I have a big experience? Why don't I get these tremendous blessings that others are receiving?

What did the father say? "All that is mine is yours" (Luke 15:31).

A lot of Christians are prodigals to the blessings of the

Lord because they do not know how to walk or live according to the Spirit. They are living in Romans 7 ("Wretched man that I am!") instead of Romans 8 ("We are children of God").

We have been blessed in Christ with every spiritual blessing in the heavenly places (Ephesians 1:3). When each of us received Jesus, the Father placed us in Christ and Christ in us. We really are among the chosen ones, members of the household of faith, part of the royal priesthood. When we have the Holy One of Israel inside, we are united with Jesus and become a tabernacle for the Holy Spirit. We are holy and blameless. And, praise God! we're blameless not only because we're forgiven; we're cleansed all the time, and we walk without a spot or blemish before the Lord.

In Christ we have redemption, the forgiveness of our sins. Some Christians are continually trying to get redeemed when they're already redeemed. Some are seeking a conversion "experience" when they are already converted. We *have* redemption.

Many, many Christians keep confessing their old natures. "Oh, God . . . I know by nature I'm sinful and unclean." Well, we *were;* but we don't need to confess our old natures anymore. We confess our newness. I'm a new creation! And we don't call ourselves unclean, because Jesus says, "You are already made clean by the word which I have spoken to you" (John 15:3).

So many of us are living like the Old Testament saints, as though our sins had not been taken away by the Lamb of God, as though his blood was not yet able to wash us and cleanse us daily. Walking under the canopy of the blood of Jesus Christ means we're cleansed and covered.

This is our heritage as believers in Jesus Christ, brothers and sisters in Jesus Christ. In Jesus we receive his Holy Spirit, a gift from God. And in him, we are heirs of heaven. All this and heaven too! We are blessed with every spiritual blessing in the heavenly places.

So it is the will of God to heal. Jesus Christ revealed the will of his Father by healing every disease and infirmity. He then died on the Cross and took our infirmities and diseases.

A pastor came to our service, heard the Word of God, and then came forward for healing. He had emphysema in his lungs. He had a diseased liver, so he was jaundiced, as well as a bad heart, high blood pressure, and bad kidneys. It was hard to imagine that the man could still walk with all this wrong with him.

I remember praying with him. In closing I said, "Now renounce your illnesses in Jesus' name."

He said, "I'll do it." So he knew what he was doing.

Then I finished the prayer with "So I lay my hands upon you in the name of Jesus. He says you shall recover, and so we know you will recover. I praise the Lord. Now you praise the Lord!" He thanked the Lord and sat down.

A person right after him was touched by the Spirit of God and knew that she was healed. He began thinking, *Now why didn't that happen to me? What's wrong with me? ... Didn't I have enough faith? There's no feeling like that in my body. I don't sense any change.*

About five minutes later, a woman sat down beside him and said, "Aren't you the one who was prayed for?"

"Yes."

"The one who had the healing?"

He said, "Oh, I don't feel so good."

"We don't go by feeling," she replied, "we go by faith. Didn't you hear? Don't you remember the message?" She began giving him the promises all over again. "Let's thank and praise the Lord for this healing."

Half an hour later he was standing outside the church when a young man came up to him and said, "You were prayed for. You have received healing."

The minister answered, "Well, I don't know. I guess I just don't have enough faith."

"Well, don't you have *some* faith?"

"Yes, I'm a Christian. I believe in the Lord."

"Don't you have any faith in healing?"

"Yes, yes."

"How big is your God?" the young man asked. "Is he big enough? The Lord is the Everlasting God. The Creator of the heavens and earth. He does not faint. He does not grow weary. His understanding is unsearchable." He began telling about the magnitude of the love and mercy of God and about his power. "Oh, let's just thank and praise the Lord for your healing!"

So he did again. Then he went home. Of course, he was bombarded in his mind all the time. He was learning to fight the fight of faith, but he had to have a lot of help along the way. He had always hated to go to bed, because he very seldom slept at night. It was always an ordeal there, tossing and turning and rolling around without sleeping. So he knelt by the bed and prayed, "Lord, you know how weak I am. And I have to say, 'Lord, help thou my unbelief.' Lord, I'm going to do one thing; I'm going to rest on one promise: 'Whatever you ask in my name, I will do it.' So Lord, I'm believing that you are doing it." Then he went to bed.

He woke up fourteen hours later. "What happened?!" he shouted, and ran into the bathroom to the mirror. The jaundice was gone. He looked different; his whole body felt like new. Within two days his blood pressure was normal and his liver, kidneys, and heart were all healed. Even the emphysema was gone. He was a whole man!

Suppose he had gone home right after my prayer. Would he have received the healing? No. He was in doubt. The Bible talks about doubt in James 1:6-8: "But let him ask in faith, with no doubting, for he who doubts is like a wave of the sea that is driven and tossed by the wind. For that person must not suppose that a double-minded man, unstable in all his ways, will receive anything from the Lord."

When we take a healing by faith, the battle is on. I know, because I've been through this many times myself. The mind, the symptoms, the feelings, what we see is still there. We've got to go up and beyond these—straight to the Word of God.

One of the best examples of this is a man only forty years old who had arthritis in both legs. He walked with two canes. He was an outdoors type, but now he had to work as a stenographer and typist. This obviously frustrated him.

We prayed for him in the name of Jesus. "Thank God for your healing," I carefully instructed.

"How can I thank God for my healing when I don't feel anything?" he complained.

I had to give him a little lecture about faith and feeling: "We don't go by what we feel. We don't go by what we see either, because faith is the evidence of things you don't see. We go by the Word of God." After speaking with him for over half an hour, we prayed again, and I said, "Now praise the Lord for your healing!"

"Lord, I don't feel a thing," he stammered, "but I'm not believing on that basis. I'm resting on the Word of God. I know that you are my Healer, and I know that you are healing me."

I said, "Good! You just keep on praising the Lord."

I met him a month later just as whole and healthy as I was. He had gained ten pounds and was as happy as a lark because now he could go out and work again.

But he said, "Oh, what a test of faith! There I was for seven days, praising and magnifying the Lord for my healing, and there was not one whit of change; the pain was still there; the stiffness was still there. There was nothing to see or feel as far as my healing was concerned. And then, on the eighth day, instead of feeling better, I began to feel worse. My legs hurt such as I had never felt before. What an ordeal it was to praise and magnify the Lord all that day when I felt so much pain! It persisted for three days.

"Then there was something like a flushing in my body, and the pain disappeared. It hasn't returned."

Such is a perfect example. Walk by faith, believe the Word of God, and then you have something that will always abide. You can rest your case on the Word.

When I was in northern Norway in 1973, I got arthritis in my right knee all the way around (I've had battles with arthritis in my back before), and soon I could not even move that leg without feeling stiff and lame. I knew that within six months I would not be able to walk on that leg; it was going that fast.

I prayed and asked the Lord to heal it, and it seemingly got worse. I had to exercise my own teaching; I had to praise and magnify the Lord. This persisted for a whole week, and as I praised, I seemed to be getting worse instead of better.

After that week, though, warmth started coming to that leg, and soon the arthritis was totally gone from my right knee. It now moves freely again. This is what the Lord expects of us: to walk by faith, to believe the Word of God, to stand on his promises.

What about medicine? How do you walk in faith if you are a diabetic who needs continued medication, for instance? I pray for many diabetics, and afterward they always ask me what to do about their medicine. I always advise, "This is something *you* have to seek from the Lord. He will let you know exactly what to do. He will guide you."

I once prayed for a diabetic man, who later testified that the next morning at the breakfast table he began wondering if he should take any insulin. He said to his wife, "I really believe the Lord was in that prayer session yesterday, and the Word of God is very plain and explicit. I believe that the Lord is healing me even though I can't feel any change in my body, so I think I'll just skip the medication for two days."

Two days went by without insulin. Then he went a whole week, then one month, and then two months without insulin. Finally he thought he should go have a check-up to see how his blood was doing. The doctor took one blood sample and came back for another one.

"No sugar, huh, doc?"

"No. There's something wrong. We'll have to take a second test," the doctor replied.

When the doctor returned, the man said, "No sugar?"

"We're going to have to take a third test. Blood sugar is incurable," he mumbled.

So they took a third test, and the man said, "No sugar?"

The doctor said, "No, I can't understand this." The third test had turned out the same as the others. The diabetes was completely healed.

A woman in Minneapolis asked me what she should do about her medicine.

"Do what seemeth right unto thee, for the Spirit of God is with thee," I paraphrased from Samuel's words to Saul in 1 Samuel 10:7.

She went home and prayed, "Lord, I'm going to wean myself from insulin." She figured out a regimen where within six months she would be off the insulin completely. And sure enough, within six months she was completely healed. The Lord healed her exactly according to her faith.

Some individuals coming into the baptism in the Holy Spirit are so set against medicine and doctors that they believe if you use any of this, you are surely confessing unbelief, and the Lord can't hear you. We need some sanctified common sense here. Doctors work in the realm of truth—natural truth. We have to live in the natural. The Lord could sustain our bodies without food, but he didn't choose to do so. Even the most "spiritual" Christian eats. And the vision of Ezekiel included "all kinds of trees for food . . . and their leaves for healing" (47:12). If you know anything about medicine, you know that much of it comes from leaves. The

Lord has given medicine, so we shouldn't fear it. It's not given by the devil, is it?

Dr. Lowell Christianson, a friend of mine, can tell of one miracle healing after another where the Lord has used him in surgery. Once a patient's heart stopped. He massaged that heart a number of times, but it would not start. He left the operating room, fell on his knees, and cried out, "Lord, what went wrong?" While he was praying, a nurse came to him and said, "Come on back. The heart started beating of its own volition."

So have a wholesome attitude about medicine. Don't have a "holy" fear against taking a pill. The Lord may use this sometime in your life. If I cut my arm very seriously, I wouldn't hesitate to go and have stitches. This natural remedy can help the healing process in my arm.

A missionary in Malaysia was retired because he had had his third heart attack, and the doctor said he'd never preach again. He came to a large service in Minneapolis. I had prayed for more than 120 people when his daughter came to me and said, "See that man over there? That's my father, Missionary Allison from Malaysia. He's retired, and he thinks because he's retired he shouldn't seek healing. Won't you go back and talk to him?"

I went back to this fine evangelical man of God. He commented, "Well, I passed the ball to somebody else."

"But wouldn't it be wonderful to be well while you're retired?" I asked.

"I suppose it would."

We sat there in the back of the auditorium, and I laid my hands on him and prayed for healing in Jesus' name.

The next morning he didn't feel any differently, but he believed the Word of God and what I had said the night before. He had been taking five or six pills a day. Now he told his daughter, "You can take these pills and give them to the Salvation Army; I don't need them anymore."

At the next meeting, he stood up and testified, "The Lord has healed my heart. He has made me whole."

A pastor in the audience found him later and said, "Would you be willing to come to my church and preach on Sunday? I have to go out of the state."

The missionary replied, "Oh, gladly. I'll come and preach."

He went on Sunday thinking he had only one message to preach, but there were two morning services plus the evening service. He preached all three times.

The following week he went to his doctor and said, "Doc, I want a complete physical because I'm going back to the mission field." The doctor gave him a thorough check-up, including his heart, and found nothing wrong. That man went back to Malaysia and served three years after his retirement, and his wife told me later that he established six new preaching stations in that time and did more effective work then than in any other segment of his life.

One particular week, he kept saying, "I don't know why, but I've got a strange feeling that we ought to go home."

"Where's home?" his wife said.

"I don't know; somewhere in the United States, I guess," he said. "But I've got a strange feeling that I've got to go home."

That Sunday morning he preached. After the noon meal, he moved to a chair and went to sleep. When his wife went to wake him up for coffee, he was dead.

She asked for an autopsy to check his heart. They could find nothing, absolutely nothing, wrong with it or any other part of his body. The Lord simply took him. He had been active in the mission field for 3½ years after he was told he would never preach again. What wonderful compensations we have in being children of God and walking in the way of the Lord!

Gertrude Tizer was a multiple sclerosis victim. She was in

a wheelchair when she prayed for and claimed a healing. She began to say, "The Lord is healing me," as she praised and magnified the Lord.

But instead of getting better, she actually got worse. Eventually she landed in a Las Vegas hospital and was deteriorating so rapidly that finally she had only one finger she could move. She kept on praising and magnifying the Lord for her healing. The doctors thought she was touched in the head; they told her family that she had a very short time to live. Her brothers sold her property and everything she had.

Then the Lord appeared to her in a vision and said, "You have been faithful to believe. Stretch out your hand." Her hand was paralyzed, but when he said it, she did it. And when she stretched out her hand, he touched it, and the power of God went through her body. She leaped out of bed and ran, praising the Lord, through the corridors of the hospital.

Not all of us are asked to go through that kind of test of faith. But when we go through some rivers (and he does want us to go through them that our faith may be tested and tried) and when we go through fires (Have you been through some fires? I know from experience the fire of persecution), the Lord says, "I will be with you."

The battlefield is in the mind. Second Corinthians 10:3-5 states, "For though we live in the world we are not carrying on a worldly war, for the weapons of our warfare are not worldly but have divine power to destroy strongholds. We destroy arguments and every proud obstacle to the knowledge of God, and take every thought captive to obey Christ."

I know the problems of the mind from a personal experience of trouble with the prostate gland. I prayed and claimed healing in the name of Jesus Christ, but for three months the symptoms persisted, that same gnawing ache and pain, that same knowing that something was radically wrong with me. I remember saying, "Lord, I know you have healed me. Praise the Lord! Your power is in my body. I know where these thoughts are coming from, but your weapons are spiritual and break down strongholds."

My healing came in a very dramatic way. I was preaching in Florida. Many people had come for prayer, and there were some dramatic healings as we prayed for the sick by laying on hands.

One morning I heard a rap on my door. When I opened it, there stood a couple named Johnson. Mrs. Johnson was crying.

"What's the trouble?" I asked.

"I have the gift of the word of knowledge. I was using it last night, if you remember," she replied.

"Yes, you told me about the woman who had the trouble in her lungs," I recalled.

"Well, I had the word of knowledge about you, I thought, with respect to your prostate gland. And I thought *Oh, no, he wouldn't have anything wrong with him like that. He looks so healthy. I must be mistaken. It must be from the devil or from the flesh.* But then I couldn't sleep all night because I didn't know if I was denying the Lord or denying the word he had given." She finally blurted, "Is this the truth?"

Excitedly I answered, "Yes, it is! I have had this trouble, and I have claimed healing. And now that the word of knowledge has come through you, I am convinced that the Lord has answered my prayers and now I have the healing in reality."

We praised and thanked the Lord for my healing. Soon a warmth came over me, and right then and there I was completely healed. I went to the doctor when I got back home, and he verified the total healing.

Fight the good fight of faith!

13

The Kingdom of God vs. the Kingdom of Satan

Don W. Basham

We are engaged in a spiritual warfare; that is one way to describe the Christian life. We are in a war with the kingdom of Satan. The battleground is not geographical; it is you and I.

Whenever discussing the subject of spiritual warfare, it is good to keep constantly in mind that Satan is a defeated foe. We minister from the standpoint of a victory already achieved. For this we must be careful to give God the praise and glory.

Several years ago when I was pastoring in Sharon, Pennsylvania, and had not yet stepped out into my present teaching ministry, a series of circumstances took place that began to make me reevaluate my own personal theology. I was a graduate of a liberal seminary and had been talked out of my belief in Satan. One of the things you learn in some theological seminaries is that Satan is a myth. There is no room in modern, "enlightened" theology for belief in a per-

---

Don W. Basham, a former commercial artist, earned the B.D. degree at Phillips Graduate Seminary and pastored Christian Churches (Disciples) in Washington, D.C., Toronto, Ontario, and Sharon, Pennsylvania. More recently he has concentrated on writing (six books, numerous articles), traveling, and teaching.

sonal adversary, Satan, and certainly not in evil spirits and demons.

Then things began to happen. Some personal attacks and some counseling sessions with persons in my church made me aware that I did have an adversary. Somebody was out to get me. That did not make me morbid, but it did make me concerned. God was allowing these things to come against me as a part of my education.

I began to restudy the Scriptures. I had to lay aside my intellectual prejudices and let the Scriptures speak for themselves. I had already done this regarding healing and the baptism in the Holy Spirit. Now I realized that the professors who had said the devil was a myth were the same men who rejected other areas of miraculous New Testament power. I discovered that if you lay aside your prejudices and let the Scriptures speak for themselves, they provide a very vivid description of our adversary Satan, his evil spirits, and how we're to deal with this particular aspect of the Christian life.

I had to make a choice. Were my seminary professors right or were the Scriptures right? I decided the Bible was right.

Church history shows that times of great spiritual prosperity in the Church are times when the Bible is exalted as the Word of God. The barren and confused spiritual times have been when the Scriptures were not recognized as the Word of God. And then I made the amazing discovery: when you come to accept the Scriptures as true and to apply New Testament methods, a very wonderful thing happens—you get New Testament results.

In the deliverance ministry we've obtained New Testament results by applying New Testament methods and principles. We've seen people instantly set free from all kinds of illnesses, frustrations, compulsions, and uncontrollable appetites that have thwarted their victory in Christ for years. Even though they're Christians—saved, baptized in the Holy Spirit, living victorious lives in many ways—they have experienced defeat continually in some area of their Christian life. Some have gone to psychiatrists, some have prayed and fasted and "reckoned the old man dead" and all of the other things a Christian should do. Still victory was not attained until they learned that there was a personal adversary and that somehow one of these demon powers had become lodged in some portion of their personality. Then, on learning of the deliverance ministry and submitting themselves to it, they were instantly set free.

In Luke 4, the account of Jesus' temptation illustrates the two kingdoms warring in our world, the Kingdom of God and the kingdom of Satan.

> And Jesus being full of the Holy Ghost returned from Jordan, and was led by the Spirit into the wilderness,
> Being forty days tempted of the devil. And in those days he did eat nothing: and when they were ended, he afterward hungered.
> And the devil said unto him, If thou be the Son of God, command this stone that it be made bread.
> And Jesus answered him, saying, It is written, That man shall not live by bread alone, but by every word of God.
> And the devil, taking him up into an high mountain, shewed unto him all the kingdoms of the world in a moment of time.
> And the devil said unto him, All this power will I give thee, and the glory of them: for that is delivered unto me; and to whomsoever I will I give it.
> If thou therefore wilt worship me, all shall be thine.
> And Jesus answered and said unto him, Get thee behind me, Satan: for it is written, Thou shalt worship the Lord thy God, and him only shalt thou serve.
> And he brought him to Jerusalem, and set him on a pinnacle of the temple, and said unto him, If thou be the Son of God, cast thyself down from hence:
> For it is written, He shall give his angels charge over thee, to keep thee:
> And in their hands they shall bear thee up, lest at any time thou dash thy foot against a stone.
> And Jesus answering said unto him, It is said, Thou shalt not tempt the Lord thy God.

And when the devil had ended all the temptation, he departed from him for a season (King James Version).

Does it say the devil departed from him for good? No, "he departed from him for a season," or as the RSV says, "He departed from him until an opportune time." Go through the ministry of Jesus and see the times when there was a concerted attempt to destroy him or to harm him in some way. Those times when Satan attacks in a more subtle and indirect way are still satanic attacks.

This passage tells us that Jesus was baptized in the Holy Ghost, then *led by the Spirit* into the wilderness to be tempted forty days by Satan. It was the Holy Spirit who set up the encounter. Whatever we receive in the Lord Jesus Christ, Satan will try to take away. Only the things we get and hold onto by faith will we keep.

We have no right to expect to be hothouse Christians, to receive the blessings of God and then be hidden and protected from all the onslaught of the enemy. This would be a complete denial of the warfare we're in. Jesus said we're not to be *of* the world, yet we are *in* the world.

Jesus' wilderness ordeal was a very private, extremely intimate encounter. No one was there except those two: Jesus and Satan.

The topic scares people today; they say, "Oh, I don't want to talk about Satan; why don't you teach about Jesus?" True, there has to be balance in these things, but we must be careful to declare the whole counsel of God. We have to share everything Jesus shared. If Jesus expected his disciples to panic at the thought of Satan, why did he tell them about this particular experience? Because that is exactly how it got into the Bible. The writers of the New Testament Gospels warn us of Satan's cunning and power.

The particular temptation we want to examine starts in verse 5:

And the devil, taking him up into an high mountain, shewed unto him all the kingdoms of the world in a moment of time.

And the devil said unto him, All this power will I give thee, and the glory of them; for that is delivered unto me; and to whomsoever I will I give it.

If thou therefore wilt worship me, all shall be thine.

We are not talking about geography here; Satan is not interested in trees and mountains, but in the people of God. Satan shows him all the kingdoms in a moment of time and says, "See, this is all mine; they belong to me; they've been delivered into my hands." The word *delivered* can also be translated *betrayed,* as when Judas betrayed Jesus to the chief priests. Satan had tremendous authority and influence while he was still the angel of light, Lucifer. He was cast down out of heaven. In the Garden of Eden he tempted Eve, and Eve tempted Adam. When they sinned and fell, the authority or dominion that they had over all the earth was betrayed into Satan's hands. Because Adam and Eve disobeyed God, the authority God had given them was added to the authority Satan had as a fallen archangel. Therefore Satan could say that all the kingdoms of the world are his. And he could give them to anyone he wanted.

The amazing thing is that Jesus did not deny Satan's claim. It is true, even today. Though Satan has been defeated by the Cross and has only squatter's rights on the earth, the fact remains that he still occupies a tremendous amount of territory that legitimately belongs to God and his people.

Who is Satan? In John 14:30 and John 12:31 Jesus refers to him as the prince or ruler of this world. In the first Scripture Jesus says, "Hereafter I will not talk much with you: for the prince of this world cometh . . . ." Jesus is acknowledging Satan for who he is.

In John 12:31 he says, "Now is the judgment of this world:

now shall the prince of this world be cast out."

In 2 Corinthians 4:4 Paul gives him another title: "The god of this world hath blinded the minds of them which believe not." All of these titles tell us who Satan is and what authority he has.

Where did Satan come from, and why did God create Satan in the first place? Did God make a mistake?

God did not create an archenemy. He created an archangel of great beauty and influence. The fall of Lucifer is found in two Scriptures in Old Testament books, Isaiah and Ezekiel. One of the accounts of the fall of Lucifer, which was Satan's original name, is in the fourteenth chapter of Isaiah. Lucifer was apparently one of the chief angels or archangels whom God created in the hierarchy of the heavenlies. (A whole heirarchy of archangels and angels exists. There is a counterpart in Satan's kingdom of evil angels and evil spirits.)

Lucifer, Gabriel, and Michael were three archangels, with many orders and suborders of heavenly hosts beneath them. *Lucifer* mean a light-bearer or light-bringer.

Isaiah 14:12-15 tells how the situation changed:

> How art thou fallen from heaven, O Lucifer, son of the morning! How art thou cut down to the ground, which didst weaken the nations!
> For thou hast said in thine heart, I will ascend into heaven, I will exalt my throne above the stars of God: I will sit also upon the mount of the congregation, in the sides of the north:
> I will ascend above the heights of the clouds; I will be like the most High.
> Yet thou shalt be brought down to hell, to the sides of the pit.

In this brief passage Lucifer five times exalts his own will against the will of the Father. This is the basic problem in the universe, the root of all sin: pride. Lucifer, an archangel with tremendous power, beauty, and authority given him by God who created him, is not satisfied with his place. He wants to exalt his own will and receive the adulation meant for God alone. He wants to exalt himself above the throne of the Most High and take the place of God. Because of that, he is cast down out of heaven and loses all his authority.

Another account of Satan's fall in the Old Testament is found in the twenty-eighth chapter of Ezekiel. The prophet has just given a lament over the "prince of Tyrus," a real, historic figure who ruled the nation of Tyre. Often, under the inspiration of the Holy Spirit, Old Testament prophets spoke not only to their own situation but also to the future, such as in the Messianic prophecies.

Here Ezekiel's description of the king of Tyre is exactly the description of Satan, his rebellion and fall. Ezekiel 28:12 says, "Son of man, take up a lamentation upon the king of Tyrus, and say unto him, Thus saith the Lord God; Thou sealest up the sum, full of wisdom, and perfect in beauty." This description of the place where Lucifer lived is another world, a heavenly kind of realm. The tremendous amount of authority, dignity, beauty, wisdom, and power he had in his original state is apparent. "Thou sealest up the sum." Lucifer was the sum of everything beautiful and good in heaven. "Thou hast been in Eden the garden of God; every precious stone was thy covering, the sardius, topaz, and the diamond, the beryl, the onyx, and the jasper, the sapphire, the emerald, and the carbuncle, and gold: the workmanship of thy tabrets and of thy pipes was prepared in thee in the day that thou was created.

"Thou art the anointed cherub that covereth; and I have set thee so: thou wast upon the holy mountain of God." This refers to Lucifer's tremendous prestige before his fall. "Thou has walked up and down in the midst of the stones of fire.

"Thou wast perfect in thy ways from the day that thou wast created, till iniquity was found in thee." The word *iniquity* means *lawlessness, rebellion.* In Isaiah Satan had wanted to rebel against the authority of God and assume for himself the worship and adoration that belonged only to God.

"By the multitude of thy merchandise they have filled the midst of thee with violence, and thou hast sinned: therefore I will cast thee as profane out of the mountain of God: and I will destroy thee, O covering cherub, from the midst of the stones of fire.

"Thine heart was lifted up because of thy beauty." There's pride. "Thou hast corrupted thy wisdom by reason of thy brightness: I will cast thee to the ground, I will lay thee before kings that they may behold thee."

These are the two Old Testament Scriptures to which Jesus referred in Luke 10 when he sent out the seventy disciples and they returned to say, "Lord, even the devils are subject unto us through thy name." Jesus made this interesting statement: "I beheld Satan as lightning fall from heaven." Then he goes on to tell the disciples, "In this rejoice not, that the spirits are subject unto you but rather rejoice, because your names are written in heaven." So Jesus himself, speaking of his preexistence with the Father, says, "I beheld Satan as lightning fall from heaven," as in the descriptions in Isaiah and Ezekiel.

Satan was cast down out of heaven. When did all this take place? Obviously it was sometime before the creation, as we understand it; at least when God made Adam and Eve and put them in the Garden of Eden, Satan was there in the form of a serpent. He tempted Eve, and this is where the whole mess got started. Without getting into a long theological discussion about when this took place, let me suggest something to you by putting two Scriptures together.

Genesis 1:1 simply says, "In the beginning God created the heaven and the earth." Many theologians say there is a great interval before verse two, which says, "And the earth was without form, and void; and darkness was upon the face of the deep." Some of the translators translate the phrase *without form* as, "And the earth was chaos; everything was chaotic, all confused and turned upside down." *Blasted* and *withered* are other terms used to describe it. Since God created the earth, and he said it was good, what happened between the time he created the world and it became chaos? In Isaiah 45:18, we see another verse about the creation. "For thus saith the Lord that created the heavens; God himself that formed the earth and made it; he hath established it, he created it not in vain, he formed it to be inhabited: I am the Lord; and there is none else."

If you put Isaiah 45:18 between Genesis 1:1 and 1:2, you come up with this: In the beginning God created heaven and earth, and though God most certainly did not intend it, the earth became a wreck and a ruin; chaos and darkness covered the face of the deep. At the point between the creation of the heaven and the earth and its becoming chaos, the rebellion of Satan came. Satan was cast out of heaven, down to the regions surrounding the earth. The effect on the earth was to blast it and to turn a perfect creation into a chaotic world. Out of that chaos the Spirit of God again began to move and bring about restoration. (I recommend a book by the late Donald Barnhouse, *The Invisible War,* which outlines in some detail this position about the great interval.)

Satan is not in hell, incidentally. He is ruling in what we call the mid-heaven, that spiritual realm somewhere between our starry heaven and the heaven where Christians go. Paul said, "we wrestle not against flesh and blood, but against principalities, against powers, against the rulers of this darkness" (Ephesians 6:12). He refers to the mid-heaven, where there is constant conflict between the warring teams. Eventually Satan will be cast into the bottomless pit along with all his evil angels and demons, but he is not there yet. He was cast down to the earth and the regions around the earth, and because of his influence theologians tell us all the earth was blasted, and God had to move again to recreate things peaceably on earth.

It is interesting when you stop and think about the Garden of Eden. What happens when you plant a garden? You create something out of a weed patch. You bring beauty and harmony into a situation where there was unrestrained wild growth before. The very fact that God planted a garden indicated that God undertook some recreating, rebuilding process after Satan blasted the earth.

This is the background for the war in which we are engaged. This warfare between the Kingdom of God and the kingdom of Satan should not be seen in terms of geography, but in terms of us, God's people. Satan is not interested in mountains; he is interested in the souls of men. Because he is the archenemy of God, he gets his greatest kick out of tormenting and trying to afflict God's people.

"We know that . . . the whole world lieth in wickedness" (1 John 5:19). Satan has dominion over the kingdoms of this earth. Many Christians and non-Christians do not like to hear about this. Some say it's an oversimplification, but I believe it. You are either in one kingdom or you are in the other. If you are not already in the Kingdom of God, if you have not been translated out of the kingdom of darkness into the Kingdom of God through his Son, if you are not a Christian, if you are not born again, if you are not a member of the Body of Christ—there is only one other kingdom you can be in. The way out of enslavement to that kingdom and that ruler is through Jesus Christ.

Satan and all the kingdoms of this world are on one hand; Christ and the Kingdom of God are on the other. Those of us who name the name of Jesus Christ as Savior have been translated out of one kingdom into the other.

The Scripture makes plain that the only way out of the world system is to get into the Kingdom of God on earth.

When Jesus came preaching that the Kingdom of Heaven was at hand at the beginning of his ministry, he was declaring war on the other kingdom. He came establishing a beachhead in the midst of the kingdoms of this world.

The warfare being fought out between these kingdoms will become increasingly apparent. Our whole nation is on a kind of psychic kick. Newspapers have reported human sacrifices to Satan in various places across the country. A fourteen-year-old boy in Tennessee was recently offered as a living sacrifice to Satan.

How can things reach that state? It is our preoccupation with the occult. It is the accumulation of these centuries during which Satan has been the ruler of this world. We have been too unaware of the supernatural aspects of his activities. We are in the end times now; all of these things are coming to the surface. He who is filthy is going to be more filthy, and he who is righteous is going to be more righteous. As the light gets brighter in the Kingdom of God, the powers of darkness will be more sharply seen for what they are. Everything is coming to a time of maturity and will be brought out into the open, as Jesus said, when those things that are whispered in secret will be shouted from the housetops.

This warfare will be fought out in supernatural terms. You cannot study this aspect of the Christian life without really becoming sober in your own thinking about the power and cunning of the enemy. He is real, vicious, and determined to destroy the people of God.

But remember, we minister from a vantage point of victory already achieved. Unless we know that victory and stand in it, Satan will chase us all around the block. Many Christians do not know what power they have in Jesus and consequently do not exercise it.

Consider how many people of God have gone on into eternity without ever knowing anything about the power of the Holy Spirit or the gifts of the Spirit. They lived on a lower level of Christian experience than God intended. They were saved and knew the Lord. Thank God, they are in heaven, but they missed a major portion of their inheritance.

We are living in a time of coming into that full inheritance, including the part that has to do with spiritual warfare and the weapons to use in it. These things have been around us for a while, but we never used them or really stopped to think about them.

On Reformation Sunday in October many of our Protestant churches sing Martin Luther's great old hymn, "A Mighty Fortress Is Our God." I sang it for years in choirs and churches; as a pastor I used to lead people in singing it. I never really paid attention to Martin Luther's message for the Body of Christ.

A mighty fortress is our God,
A bulwark never failing:
Our helper he amid the flood
Of mortal ills prevailing.
But still our ancient foe
Doth seek to work us woe;
His craft and power are great,
And armed with cruel hate;
On earth is not his equal.

Luther knew what it was to fight the prince of darkness and wrote about it in his hymns.

Did you know that eighty-five percent of the daily newspapers in America run daily horoscopes? Why? Because it sells newspapers. You think horoscopes are harmless? They are instruments in the hands of Satan. The signs of the zodiac are one of the most popular interior-decorating motifs in our country today.

When I was working on *Deliver Us from Evil,* one of my editors sent me a clipping from the *New York Times.* It was the story of a young man in New York City who with some of his friends began to get in touch with some demon entities by means of the drug route. The young man instructed his friends to tie him hand and foot and dump him in the river. He wanted to commit suicide because he had been told that once he died he would be captain of fifty demon spirits in the other world.

This sort of thing we could not possibly have conceived a few years ago. People say, "We never used to hear about evil spirits, demons, deliverance, and Satan; why is all this suddenly coming up in our day?" Well, we never used to hear about a lot of things. We never used to hear about campus rebellion and race riots and the drug scene. It is the time in which we live.

Just as Satan is pouring out his counterfeit Pentecost, God is moving by his Spirit, pouring out his Spirit on all flesh. More and more will come out in the open. Warfare between the two kingdoms will be more and more supernatural. Satan is a lot fancier and more dramatic with his supernatural stuff than the gifts of the Holy Spirit. Satan will show off; the Holy Ghost will not. Look what he told Jesus, "If you are the Son of God, why not jump off this Temple, just fly down like an angel, and show the world who you are?" Jesus was genuinely tempted. He had the power and he knew it, but he said, "It is written, Thou shall not tempt the Lord thy God."

In the fullness of time, Jesus did do what Satan defied him to do. He did defy gravity when he walked on the water that stormy night when he came to his disciples in the boat. But there he did it in the will of God to demonstrate a series of principles. He would not use that kind of power to show off.

When I was in New Zealand, I stayed with a young pastor who had ministered to a young woman who had been sold as a bride to Satan. She had become a witch and had gone through a marriage ceremony to Satan. This pastor shared with me the horrors that came out during the deliverance. One will help make you aware that we live in a time like no other, and we can never return to the time when everything was nice and quiet.

They took this young woman home from a service one night and, as they were walking toward the house, she said to the minister and his associate, "Now don't be surprised, but when you step into my yard, you're going to feel cold. That goes with the stuff I've been in." He took the woman by the arm and turned into the sidewalk to her door. It was like stepping into a refrigerator. The temperature dropped thirty or forty degrees right there, even though it was a warm summer evening.

When they reached the door, he said, "Give me your key and I'll let you in."

"You don't have to do that," she replied. "I'll just walk right on through." Right before his eyes he saw the woman start to go through that wooden door. She was halfway through when he grabbed her by the elbow and pulled her back. She just laughed and said, "Oh, we do that sort of thing all the time." It took a period of some months before this woman was completely delivered from all those influences, even though she had given her life to Christ.

One night when she was having difficulty, she called the parsonage. The minister was not home. She talked with his wife. "I'm being harassed by the enemy and I'm fearful," she said. "I wonder if I could come over, or could the pastor come over and pray with me?"

His wife said, "Well, he's out now, but why don't you come over here and wait till he comes back."

She hesitated and said, "Well, I don't know how I'd get there; I don't have cabfare, and it's about seven miles from here . . . . But if you'll let me come on the wings of darkness, I'll be there in thirty seconds."

The minister's wife said, "No, no, don't do that! You take a cab; we'll pay the fare."

Later she rode around town with the pastor and would say,

"See that woman? She's a witch. See that man? He's a warlock." Earlier, when she had gone through the ritual of selling herself to be married to Satan, a silver ring had appeared supernaturally on the third finger of her left hand. When these Christians finally reached the point where they were going to deliver this girl, they realized that part of the problem was this ring. The pastor and his associate prayed with her, trying everything they knew to get that ring off her finger. It was as if it were glued there. They just could not get it off. Finally, they just stood back and commanded the ring to come off in the name of Jesus, and it flew off across the room, hit the wall, and landed on the floor. With that, the girl was set free.

I share this sort of thing simply to illustrate that we are in a war. We need not be scared if we are citizens in the Kingdom of God. But we do need to know what power the enemy has. We should be aware of the host of evil spirits spreading havoc in the Body of Christ because of the ignorance of God's people. God is restoring to the Church everything that happened in the New Testament. Paul wrote in Philippians 4:19, "My God shall supply all your need according to his riches in glory by Christ Jesus." Everything we have and need is offered to us by the Lord. Every ministry that was effective in the New Testament Church is being restored today—the baptism in the Holy Spirit, the healing ministry, and now the deliverance ministry. Everything that happened then is happening now. Everything that was needed then, we need now. The early Church needed salvation, healing, and baptism in the Holy Spirit . . . and they needed deliverance too.

Jesus came to earth as Savior, Healer, Baptizer, and Deliverer. He is doing the same thing today.

14

Coming Alive

Winston I. Nunes

I often go to my library and pick out a certain book to read, only to discover I have read it already. But no matter how many times I read the Scripture, it is always new—because it is the Word of God. "Heaven and earth shall pass away," Jesus said, "but my words shall not pass away" (Matthew 24:35 King James Version). God has magnified his Word above even his name, according to Psalm 138:2. Genesis says, "In the beginning God created the heaven and the earth. And the earth was without form and void; and darkness was upon the face of the deep. And the Spirit of God moved upon the face of the waters" (1:1,2).

Yet that was not enough. No matter how long the Spirit moved, the earth still was without form, void, and watery. (Never settle for the moving of the Holy Spirit alone.) What happened? What changed the situation?

"And God said . . . ."

When the Word of God came, something happened. "God

Winston I. Nunes has been pastor of Toronto's Faith Temple for more than fifteen years. A native of Trinidad, he has lived in Canada since attending seminary in Winnipeg. He recently organized a charismatic communion of Toronto clergy; he is also an officer in the Elim Missionary Assemblies.

said, Let there be light: and there was light" (1:3). According to Hebrews 11:3, "We understand that the worlds were framed by the word of God." Without the Word, nothing is made.

We are born again not because we shook some preacher's hand, or prayed some prayer of repentance, or came to the front of a church. We are born again because of the incorruptible seed, "the word of God, which liveth and abideth forever" (1 Peter 1:23). We are healed because he sends his Word to heal and deliver us from all our afflictions.

"In the beginning was the Word, and the Word was with God, and the Word was God . . . . All things were made by him" (John 1:1,3). The Word is called "him." The Word is a *person—Jesus Christ.* The next verse does not say, "In him was blessing." It does not say, "In him was light." It does not say, "In him was love." The Scripture says, "In him was *life!*"

The problem in the world is not love. The world says what we need is love, more love, but that's nonsense. Greater love is impossible after "God so loved the world, that he gave his only begotten Son." What greater love can we imagine than the Son coming forth into humanity with all the limitations, yet providing for us a glorious redemption through his blood? He was "made in the likeness of sinful flesh" (Romans 8:3). "He took not on him the nature of angels; but he took on him the seed of Abraham . . . to be made like unto his brethren, that he might be a merciful and faithful high priest in things pertaining to God" (Hebrews 2:16,17). And he can "be touched with the feeling of our infirmities," because "he was in all points tempted like as we are, yet without sin" (Hebrews 4:15).

So the Scripture says, "In him was life." The problem with people is that they are dead and dissipated. Their problem is not lying, cheating, or getting drunk on Saturday night. It is that they are dead spiritually, out of relationship with God. They may be alive socially, intellectually, financially, and many other ways, but in the most vital area of their lives they are dead. "The wages of sin is death; but the gift of God is eternal life" (Romans 6:23). Jesus did not say, "I came to give love," but rather, "I am come that they might have life, and that they might have it more abundantly" (John 10:10). Don't I believe in love? Of course I do, but let's keep things in the right order. John is the man who wrote of love. However, we must read into the second, third, and fourth chapters of his epistle before we discover God is love. In the first chapter he says, "God is light, and in him is no darkness at all" (verse 5). At the beginning of his Gospel he says of Jesus, "In him was life; and the life was the light of men" (1:4).

We are living in the day when all sorts of philosophies are coming to us not only from our own civilization but also out of the East. They promise "light." But God's initial and ultimate gift to each of us is life. And what we need in these days is a greater infusion of the life of God, which comes to us by his Spirit.

As many as received the Lord Jesus Christ, "to them gave he power to become the sons of God" (John 1:12). The story of the birth of John the Baptist illustrates this power. Zacharias and Elizabeth are praying for a baby, but they get too old. Finally an angel of the Lord appears to Zacharias. The first thing the angel says is "Fear not, Zacharias: for thy prayer is heard; and thy wife Elizabeth shall bear thee a son" (Luke 1:13). But some of the best *praying* people are ironically the most *unbelieving* people. Zacharias, despite all his praying, says, "Whereby shall I know this? for I am an old man, and my wife well stricken in years" (verse 18). The angel has to identify himself as Gabriel and says, "Behold, thou shalt be dumb, and not able to speak . . . because thou believest not my words, which shall be fulfilled in their season" (verse 20).

Believe it or not! "If we believe not, yet he abideth faithful: he cannot deny himself" (2 Timothy 2:13). "Shall **their** unbelief make the faith of God without effect? God forbid!" (Romans 3:3,4). When God says he'll do something, neither you nor I nor anyone in the universe with unbelief is going to stop him. "Hath he said, and shall he not do it? or hath he spoken, and shall he not make it good?" (Numbers 23:19). "There hath not failed one word of all his good promise" (1 Kings 8:56).

Zacharias did not believe—but they still had the baby! It was an intervention of God. The Word of God had been spoken.

I thank God for Thomas. I can now praise God for all false prophets and all doubters. (I'm beginning to thank God for everything.) Thomas said, "It's all right for you people to tell me Jesus is risen, but unless I can put my finger . . . ."

Jesus appeared and said to Thomas, "Reach hither thy finger, and behold my hands; and reach hither thy hand, and thrust it into my side" (John 20:27). He had literally and actually come out of the tomb.

There's nothing to fear in the future, because Jesus Christ is in control of the future. Have we ever read when Jesus was frightened? When Pilate said to him, "Why don't you answer me? Don't you know I hold your fate in my hands?" did Jesus' knees begin to knock? Did he say, "You would have no power against me at all except that the devil is giving you this power"? No! He said, "Thou couldest have no power at all against me, except it were given thee from above" (John 19:11). It was the *Father's* power! The Lord's prayer ends, "Thine is the kingdom, and the power, and the glory, for ever" (Matthew 6:13).

If Jesus Christ has all power in heaven and earth, nothing is going to happen contrary to his will. I have three favorite verses of Scripture on this topic. The first is Romans 8:28: "We know that all things work together for good to them that love God, to them who are the called according to his purpose."

The next is 1 Peter 3:13—"Who is he that will harm you, if

ye be followers of that which is good?" Nothing can harm us, no matter how many enemies we have and how they hate us. Jesus never said we could be harmed by our enemy hating us, but rather by hating him in return.

The third verse I like is 2 Corinthians 13:8—"We can do nothing against the truth, but for the truth." After Paul was in Philippi, some false preachers came with two objectives. One was to discredit Paul's mission; the other was to discredit him. But Paul knew that nothing could hurt the Word of God. Some "preach Christ of contention, not sincerely, supposing to add affliction to my bonds . . . . What then? notwithstanding, every way, whether in pretence, or in truth, Christ is preached; and I therein do rejoice" (Philippians 1:16,18).

Perhaps some minister demonstrates tremendous gifts, great eloquence, and marvelous signs—and we find out he's a crook. We wonder, "How could a crook like that . . . how could he?" God doesn't confirm the crook, but he does confirm his truth, and it doesn't matter who says it.

At the Last Supper, Jesus happened to mention swords, and the disciples informed him that they had two of them. What if Jesus had said, "Station one man with a sword at this door, and station the other fellow with a sword at that door, because one of you is a crook, and he's going out to betray me. And you know what's going to happen: if he gets out that door, the whole business is going to blow up"?

Peter would have responded, "Oh, just try and get out this door! I'll let him have it!"

But they didn't get that message; Jesus withheld the information, and Judas slipped out to make a mess of the whole situation. He betrayed the Lord and got him crucified. If only they'd known, they could have killed Judas, saved the Lord from the Cross—and sent us all to hell!

The next time we think something is working for bad and hurting the truth, we ought to remember that Christ is building his Church. God never gives the church to the pastor; he gives the pastor to the church. When he ascended, he gave to the church apostles, prophets, evangelists, pastors and teachers. Pastors sometimes become alarmed: "What will happen to my church?" If it is *their* church, I hope it blows up! It is Christ's church, they are his people, they are washed in his blood, and he's coming for them. Pastors who say "my congregation" are claiming what is Christ's for themselves. We happen to be the other shepherds through whom he is ministering to them.

Acts 1:1 mentions "all that Jesus *began* both to do and teach." He still teaches through his ministries today—in order that the Church of Jesus Christ may hear his voice and be built up in a most holy way.

One night when I was preaching on the mission field, everything went wrong. The choir couldn't sing; the congregational singing was dead; and when I got up to preach, I put my right foot in my mouth, and that didn't work, so I took it out and put my left foot in. Finally I started leading a chorus and said, "Everybody who wants to be healed, come forward." One hundred twenty people came.

I went down and laid my hands on the first person and prayed. No liberty, no anointing, no quickening; even as my prayer left my mouth, you could sense it hitting the ceiling and bouncing back. I prayed for two or three others. I asked the choir to sing a song; they fizzled out. I was dying with frustration. I prayed, "Lord, what is wrong?"

The Lord replied, "Nothing is wrong."

"Hold on; there's no liberty in the singing, I couldn't preach, and I have absolutely no quickening to pray. What's wrong?"

"I don't heal people because the choir sings well," the Lord said. "I don't heal people because you find it easy to pray. I heal them because I took their infirmities and bore their sicknesses."

So I said, "Thank you, Lord." And I prayed for the other

110. It was still dead; I had no liberty. But would you believe that 120 people were healed in that meeting?

I don't like that kind of thing, because I couldn't take the credit! But Matthew 8:17 quotes Isaiah as saying, "Himself took our infirmities, and bare our sicknesses." We can be healed because he has already done it. It happened two thousand years ago.

The same is true for salvation. I had the privilege of being a chaplain for a year in a terrible prison with 350 awful criminals. One fellow was the worst; the commissioner had said, "Don't let him out until he goes feet first; he's too bad." They had done everything to him—solitary confinement, cat-o'-nine-tails, and everything else they knew.

They brought him into the meeting after all the other prisoners were in. Two guards stood beside him at the back so they could take him out quickly if he started trouble. But when he heard the Word of God, tears ran down his face, and he said, "God be merciful to me, a sinner." God saved him.

Can a man so bad be saved so quickly? Yes! On the Cross Jesus said, "It is finished." The work of redemption is completed. And when men trust in the blood of Jesus Christ and believe that he's alive to save them, God does it immediately. When he brings us alive in him, there is no stopping him.

Part Seven

The Holy Spirit Worshiping

15

Into the Holy of Holies

E. Judson Cornwall

God doesn't want just us; he wants us as true worshipers. He accepts us as we are in order to make us just what he wants. His mercy and grace will take us as hellbent sinners—defiled, twisted, deformed, full of all types of problems and internal evil—and start a process that will take probably the biggest part of eternity to complete. He changes us from what we were to what he is.

By the exercise of self-will man pulled himself from the image of God, deformed himself from the glory of God, defiled himself from the holiness of God, and has been on a downward trend from that day to this.

Some hold the concept that we are getting better and better, and eventually we will get so great that God will come down and live with us. That is the aim of religion. But revealed truth, revealed faith, shows that God saw man getting worse and worse, and so he came down to enable man to get better.

We do not get better by our own efforts—"not by works of righteousness which we have done, but according to his mer-

---

E. Judson Cornwall is a veteran pastor of more than twenty-seven years who presently concentrates on teaching and evangelism.

cy he saved us, by the washing of regeneration ..." (Titus 3:5 King James Version). The processes of God are not just to enable us to enjoy God more but to enable God to enjoy us more. He is changing us so that he can relate to us as well as vice versa.

The Tabernacle is a pattern to understand some of the basic stages in relating to God. God did his best to make it comfortable for people to approach him. He allowed the Tabernacle to be made out of materials they themselves could create. He allowed them to bring something they were comfortable with as they came to worship, and that became part of the worship at the brazen altar.

Then when the priest came one step closer to God from the outer court to the holy place, he was again allowed to bring something that was comfortable: he brought fire with him from the brazen altar to light the lamp and the incense in the holy place.

In the holy place we learn something more about the close relationship available to us in God. The burning altar speaks to us of the Cross. What a beautiful efficacy for sin has been made through Christ at Calvary! At the laver we learn something of the washing of the water by the Word. Thank God for the sanctifying work of the Spirit of God. But that is the outer court, a long way from God.

Although you thought you met God at the Cross, God is not on that burning, blazing altar. God is in his holy Temple. Although you thought you met God in the Word, he is not there. He is on the throne.

And so we come closer; we step through the second veil. The first veil speaks of unity, of Jesus the Way. The second veil stands between the outer court and the holy place.

Stepping through the second veil, which is Jesus the Truth, we start learning the truth about the truth about the Truth. The Scriptures reveal the truth about the Truth. Doctrine is

171

putting truth together so that we can understand the Bible. Doctrine is to teach us about the truth. Theology is for telling us the truth about doctrine. So we have the truth about the truth about the Truth.

However, there comes a time when, instead of knowing the truth in the fourth dimension, we start to know Jesus and ourselves. Then, in coming into the holy place with its ministry of the lampstand, we receive his Spirit and his truth and his gifts. We have light that we never had before. Spiritual ministry requires this spiritual illumination.

From the lampstand to our left we turn to the golden table, the table of communion, the table of his presence. Eating the pierced cake of unleavened bread, we learn something of fellowshiping in Jesus.

Probably the Church restored the brazen altar about the time of Luther, and during the time of the Wesleys the laver was reestablished. Perhaps about the time of the rise of the Pentecostals the candlestick was reestablished. I think the present charismatic movement has restored the ministry of the golden table. We are learning to fellowship with Jesus Christ. There are no big or little, no high priests or lesser priests. We are not interested in what department you belong to, not concerned at all about education or lack of it. We want to know only one thing: do you feed on Jesus the Truth? If so, then you are my brother; you are my sister. We are learning something about the lordship of Jesus Christ and the authority he has in each of us.

Yet, even though the Pentecostals thought they had found God in the candlestick, and although we charismatics think we have found God at this marvelous golden table, God is neither in the lampstand nor on the table. All of these are simply the provisions of God to change us.

The golden altar of incense was in direct line with the brazen altar and the laver, but it was positioned right in front of the veil. Tradition tells us the veil was four feet thick, but that was true only of the Temple veil. The Tabernacle had only a single linen veil. You could see shadows and receive divine energies through it. When God designed the Tabernacle in the wilderness, he didn't separate himself from his people as he did when they built the Temple.

God is beckoning us from the table to the altar. There seems to be a different relationship between the table and altar, for it is very difficult to become a partaker of Jesus Christ without responding in worship. To see him, to taste him is to love him.

I am a great believer in getting people to accept Jesus by letting them see him. Reveal Jesus, and the altars will have penitents. We can preach sin, death, hell, damnation, and destruction every day from now until it happens, and we won't get them to the altar. It is not a scared prayer that is going to change people; it is seeing Jesus and sensing his love.

We come to the golden altar and begin fellowshiping first with one another and secondly with Jesus. We want to respond to him, and the golden altar is where we do it. Here is where the incense is offered. Incense is a compound of many different fragrances, but in order to release them it is necessary to grind and blend and bind. Those who seem to exude such a gentle love, those toward whom we find our spirit gravitating, usually have been beaten. It is part of the process of God to produce a fragrance. To have life more abundantly often means that he must release us from the less abundant aspects of life, so when he seems to pound us and bind us together and set us on fire, we begin to exude prayer, starting with worship and thanksgiving and then prayer and supplication.

We are still on our side of the veil and God is on his side, but we are closer than we have ever been. We are close enough that our incense is getting through to God. Prayer reaches God as a sweet smell.

On the other side of the veil is the real reason for the Tabernacle. God has declared to the people who rejected him,

"I will walk among you; I will dwell with you; I will be your God, and you will be my people. But I have placed myself in such an accommodating position that only you who choose to come will come. I will never come out and threaten you."

Inside the holy place is the mercy seat. God said, "I will meet with thee, and I will commune with thee from above the mercy seat" (Exodus 25:22). All divine communication comes from the mercy seat. However, it was not necessary to go inside the holy of holies to hear. You could hear through the veil.

So the question is asked, "What value is there in going on into the holy of holies if the worship from the golden altar goes in to God and the communication from him comes out to men? Why get any closer?"

That is the same argument we got from the brazen altar: "My sins have been forgiven; why go any further?" I have heard the same at the laver: "I have been made holy and pure; why go any further?" The reason I want to go further is because God is neither in the fire nor in the water; God is on the throne! The goal of my heart and spirit is to see God.

In our present bodies we can never come into the full revelation of God. Moses had beautiful communication with God through the fire, and then in the cloud, but he said, "O God, I've got to see you. I must come closer."

And God said to Moses, "I can't let you see me totally, but I will let you see me. I will put my hand over you as I pass by, and when I have passed by, I will lift my hand that you may see my afterglow."

Paul, speaking of Jesus, said, "Which in his times he shall shew, who is the blessed and only Potentate, the King of kings, and Lord of lords; who only hath immortality, dwelling in the light which no man can approach unto; whom no man hath seen, nor can see; to whom be honour and power everlasting. Amen" (1 Timothy 6:15,16).

Moses was told, "You can't see me totally." Paul says to Timothy, "Let's set the record straight. God dwells in an aura of light that is so totally spiritual that it is destructive to that which is totally physical."

But after the death of Jesus, the veil of the Temple was torn. A way into God's presence was made available. Scripture tells us we should draw nearer—boldly, with a pure heart, with a pure conscience, with a cleansed body. There is an access. The most normal approach to God is a veiled approach. God is behind the veil for our sakes until such time as we are totally transformed into his image.

To the priest entering the holy of holies, the most obvious thing is the light, the glory which is the glory of God. How fearsome to approach it from our side! But how glorious it is on God's side! We see the light, that is, Jesus. We see the beauty in him.

Epilogue

A Layman
and the Holy Spirit

Pat Boone

Pat Boone—his name appeared on Billboard's *charts during the 1950s for more than 200 consecutive weeks, an all-time record. He was the youngest performer ever to host a network TV show. Thirteen gold records (one million sales each) came his way, and total sales of more than 45 million records.*

Yet by the late sixties he faced the twin specters of bankruptcy and a disintegrating marriage. At that point, the Holy Spirit brought a dramatic turnaround (as told in his book A New Song*). Since then, Pat Boone has been refreshingly candid about his spiritual life, whether in his own live shows, in guest appearances, or in his recording, film-making, and writing. The following collection of personal stories and thoughts give a glimpse into his everyday walk in the Spirit.*

When I was in a circus movie a few years ago, I had to go thirty feet up a rope hand over hand, swing out on a trapeze, make some circles—it was to be quite a scene. We were practicing in an empty Twentieth Century Fox studio, a professional trapeze artist and I, and I would swing from a table only two or three feet above the ground. I got to be pretty good at it.

Then we went to England to do the movie in the big top. The day came when we were to rehearse and shoot. I went up that rope, thirty feet above the ground, feeling real proud of myself. The circus guys were amazed that an actor could do it.

That platform seemed awfully tiny and shaky. These two professionals said, "Okay, off you go!" Oh, man!

But I had to do it. It was like swinging off the end of the world. It seemed like five minutes just getting out there.

Then I came back. My teacher hadn't taught me to pull the bar up to my waist on the backswing in order to pass the platform. So when I swung back the first time, it hit me right in the back! I couldn't figure out what had happened. I swung out again and came back, and they were yelling, "Pull up, pull up!"

But I was completely disoriented, and with each swing I was losing momentum. Finally I just came to the point where my only choice was to drop into the net.

After that first time, it wasn't so bad anymore. I'd experienced just about everything that could happen to me. I'd been embarrassed. I'd been frightened out of my mind. I had dropped and been caught by the net.

That incident parallels, for me, some of the excitement of the Spirit-filled life. Sometimes, if we are to experience what God wants us to experience, we have to leave the platform and swing out there, believing that he's there. And of course, some of us make a mistake. We hit the platform, maybe several times, and eventually we have to drop, but then there's the net; the Lord catches us. So we get up and try again. After we risk stepping off that small platform, we learn how to live on a plane higher than everyone around us. It really is an exciting life filled with adventure and danger.

I've met some people who have just recently come into the fullness of the Spirit. They're still on cloud nine. Everything is just like a honeymoon. I hesitate to tell them, "Look, fasten your seat belt, because some bumps are coming. But at least God has given you the power, and he's going to see you through all of those bumps if you'll just hang on."

Hanging on is important. While we were filming, there was some aerial work which a stunt man from Rome was to do. He had just been working with Richard and Elizabeth Burton on *Cleopatra,* and he'd not only been doubling for Richard Burton for stunts, but he had evidently been spending some time with him off camera and was in none too good shape. I could tell he was more scared than I was; he had to work without a shirt, and you could see his soft stomach just shaking. He told me confidentially that he had never done trapeze work before, but he needed the money, so he had said he could do it since he was used to doing other kinds of stunts.

Well, we got all ready to do the day's shooting. He went up the ladder to that platform and swung out—and the same thing happened to him that had happened to me. He had to drop into the net. The director and everyone looked around and said, "Is this the guy we're paying all that money to do the stunt work?"

"My pants are too tight," he said. So they gave him another pair of pants, but the same thing happened.

Finally he had to give up, and it looked as if the whole day's shooting and many thousands of dollars would go down the drain. So I said, "Look, let me do it. I've done it close to the ground, and I've been up there."

"No, if something happens to you," they said, "not only would the day's shooting be gone, but our movie would be finished. That's why we brought in this stunt man."

"Yeah, but he can't do it." I said. "Look, I guarantee that I'm not going to let go of that handle. It would take an acetylene torch to get my hands off that thing." We got the scenes on film, and I was quite thrilled to do my own stunt work.

There's probably a parallel there too. If we hold on once we have come into the Spirit-filled walk and don't let anybody or anything pry our hands out of his, he's going to see us through, and we'll get the job done. But we're going to be tempted and frightened. It will be like the time Peter was walking on the water. He's out there in front of all his friends. He's also with Jesus, of course, but then he sees the waves and the wind and all the physical surroundings. His rational mind takes over, and he says, "Hey, I can't be doing this!" So, bloonk! there he goes. He's sinking.

Jesus comes over and says, "O you of little faith, how long will you doubt?" We've got to keep our eyes on Jesus and hang in there.

As I said in my book, I don't know where I've been all my life! I know heaven's going to be fun. I never used to have any idea about heaven. I only thought about it in terms of church. I remember so clearly sitting there in the pew when I was nine or ten years old, my mind wandering . . . and I'd think to myself, *Hmmm, a million years . . . ten million years of church . . . and heaven has only begun.* I don't mind admitting that I was not too thrilled with the idea.

My frame of reference was so narrow then. Now, of course, I realize I'm going to be in heaven with Catholics, Baptists and Methodists and all kinds of Pentecostal people, Quakers, Jews, black people, Chinese people, Puerto Rican people—all brothers, precious to God.

In Little Rock, Arkansas, something special happened to me. An older black bellhop was assigned to show me to my hotel room. I noticed his nametag said "Tom," and as we were walking toward the room he said, "You know, I'm glad to get to do this for you, because you're my brother."

I almost cried. I said, "Tom, you're my brother too, and I hope I get to carry your bags someday."

God is bringing us together in the unity of the Spirit. We used to talk about it in my church, and we thought it could only be accomplished after everybody came to see things our way. But unity can be accomplished by his Spirit as we individually submit ourselves to him. We cannot put the barriers or limits on our submission, but just let him take us gently, step by step, day by day.

In 1973 our family went to Israel to do a television special—a rather unusual one which traced the steps of Christ from Bethlehem to the Sea of Galilee, Tiberias, Capernaum, through the synagogue there, then through Jericho and the wilderness into Jerusalem, to Golgotha, and finally to the Garden Tomb.

At the end of the taping, the crew went home, and Shirley, the girls, and I stayed on for a few days of sightseeing. Finally on the last afternoon, we went back to a place we wanted to see again, the Garden Tomb. Somehow we felt we hadn't really seen it well enough while taping the musical number; we hadn't had time to absorb quietly what God had for us in that place. We went back in the late afternoon.

As we stooped in order to enter, I sensed the message: he is alive! It absorbed my whole being. It seemed significant that one could not go in or come out of the tomb without bowing down and humbling himself. We all six sat there in that little tomb and looked at the slab where we believe Jesus' body lay. It was a dark, cloudy afternoon outside. As we sang, worshiped, and wept there, singing the hymns we've always loved, they had a new depth and meaning. It was dark; it was cold. We sensed not only what it must have been like, but for me it had a feeling of familiarity, as if I'd been there before. I tried to figure that out.

Shirley and the girls were having the same feeling. The reason was that we went in there with Jesus. Every living human being went in there; that was our destiny. When the stone was rolled shut, we all were locked in for eternity.

But that day as we felt the bleakness, the barrenness, the finality of it, we also had the sense of another Presence. It wasn't just a body on a slab, it was a powerful Presence, as when that stone rolled back and that still figure rose, dropped his burial clothes, and walked out into the beautiful garden. We said in our spirits, reaching out, "Jesus! Wait for us. Take us with you. Don't leave us in here!" And Jesus turned and, with a smile, held out his hand and said, "Come." We realized that is his invitation to the world. "I've made the way. Come."

We had the deepest sense of the *right* of Jesus to say, "I am the Way—yes, and the Truth, and the Life. No one can get to the Father except by means of me" (John 14:6 Living Bible). I'd always thought of that in the future tense, that someday we would come, because of Jesus, to the Father. But the tenth chapter of Hebrews says, "And so, dear brothers, *now* we may walk right into the Holy of Holies where God is, because of the blood of Jesus" (verse 19). This is the fresh, new, life-giving way which Christ has opened up for us by tearing the curtain, his human body, to let us into the holy presence of God. Jesus says, "No man comes to the Father but by me." That means *now!* We can come into the presence of God, the very holy of holies that was denied to everyone except the high priests. Jesus is our High Priest, and we are in him. Let us go right in with pure hearts to God himself, truly trusting him to receive us, because we have been sprinkled with Christ's blood to make us clean, and our bodies have indeed been washed.

I keep being reminded of the third chapter of John, where a religious leader came to Jesus at night. This happens to me often—people who have publicly taken a strong position against me and what I believe and have experienced come to me privately to ask a few more questions. They have seen something they can't shrug off. They get an inner urge to come back, to reinvestigate.

I keep showing them how Jesus told Nicodemus that the

Holy Spirit is like the wind, and that no man knows where he's been, where he's coming from, or where he's going next. So it is with everyone born of the Spirit.

Some of my Church of Christ brethren have asked me about that. "Do you mean that a Christian is supposed to be unpredictable?"

There was a time when I would have said no. But I've had to change my outlook, because so many of the really dynamic Christians that I now know are so utterly unpredictable, including myself. I'm often asked on television, "What lies ahead for Pat Boone?"

My answer is "I don't know. I really don't. I'm just led a day at a time."

If anyone would have told me two or three years ago that I would be asked to write the foreword for a book by an Orthodox Jewish rabbi, I wouldn't have believed it. But this is just what happened. I asked Arthur Katz, Messianic Jew, to come to our home and speak to a gathering of people from the entertainment and professional field, all Jews. About seventy of them were Orthodox Jews while the other thirty were Christian Jews just sprinkled through the crowd.

Arthur Katz spoke quite forcefully, and some people began to challenge him. One man named Israel said to him, "You don't have the right to call yourself a Jew!"

"Why do you say that?"

"Because you're a Christian! You're something else," he said.

Art answered, "I'm more Jewish than I ever was. More proud of my background. More in tune with the God of Abraham, Isaac, and Jacob than I've ever been in my life."

But the man couldn't see it. It started to get hot.

About this time I heard footsteps in the kitchen. A latecomer had just arrived. I looked, saw who it was, and said, "Folks, why don't we wait just a minute, because maybe it's time we heard from a rabbi." There was a gasp in the room. A rabbi in this setting? Some looked anxiously at the other door, thinking maybe they ought to beat it, when in walked Michael Esses.

I said, "I want you to know Rabbi Michael Esses, also a Messianic Jew, completed in the Messiah Jesus." Another gasp.

Of course, after a little while, they challenged his right to call himself a rabbi. Mike's reply was beautiful. "I do not represent a Jewish congregation at this time, but you cannot take away my rabbinical training, my knowledge, the fact that I am a teacher. I am, in fact, still a rabbi in a general sense, in the true sense."

The meeting lasted until three o'clock in the morning, when I invited everyone to come back two days later. About thirty or forty returned and about midnight we baptized nine Jews in our swimming pool.

It seemed like something right out of the book of Acts. The Acts of the Holy Spirit are still going on. We call the fifth New Testament book The Acts of the Apostles, and of course the apostles were involved as the men who had to step out in faith, but it's primarily the work of the Holy Spirit. The book is a history of what the Holy Spirit was doing. Many of us see that this was the pattern to last throughout the ages for all men who have the faith to see it, to receive it, to ask to be used in the same way by the same Holy Spirit.

Since then I've written the foreword to Mike's book. In fact, I often wear my shalom pin and tell everyone I'm Jewish. I'm an adopted Jew.

People say, "How can you be an adopted Jew?"

I say, "Well, I'm glad you asked." We get into some very interesting discussions on planes and in other places. As time goes on, I'm getting some feedback from these discussions, so I know God has created this opportunity for a reason. The Bible says to be ready to give an answer to those who ask you. Some Christians want to confront and corner everyone (and maybe for some people that is a ministry), but I just sort of live along and wait for somebody to ask me, and the talks and sharing that result take up most of my time as it is. I always try to be ready for the moment when someone questions me. Being ready takes time—being prayed up, well-versed in Scripture, having right relationships with other people, and staying sensitive to the leading of the Holy Spirit. It seems to work out more gracefully that way.

Because of the Holy Spirit working, some entertainers have come to me with questions. I've had great discussions with Jonathan Winters, Doris Day, Bob Goulet and his wife, Carol Lawrence, Zsa Zsa Gabor, Lucille Ball, Elvis Presley a couple of times, and other people you would know.

One night Bob Goulet came backstage at the Forum and said, "Boone," (this was in front of Red Buttons, Jimmy Cahn, Greg Morris, and Johnny Mathis) "how do you get the Holy Spirit in ya?"

"Well," I said, "Bob, you just ask. Jesus said the Father will give the Holy Spirit to those who ask."

He said, "No, I want to know he's in there. I've got some things in there that I don't like. I want to get them changed." That's the kind of guy Bob is—direct and blunt and to the point. "Bob," I said, "can you imagine God himself coming to dwell in you by his Holy Spirit and you not knowing it? His not changing anything? Not rocking the boat? Never!"

About that time Red Buttons chimed in, "Say, I'm doing a joke about you in my act."

"Yeah?"

"Yeah, it gets a big laugh."

"What is it?"

"Well, I tell people I went swimming at Pat Boone's house, and he dunked me three times."

I said, "It gets a big laugh, huh?"

"Yeah."

"Keep telling it," I said—because this means that not only he knows what's going on, but so do his audiences.

More than one Church of Christ minister has come to me

and said, "Look, I am a believer. I am a Christian. I have been baptized. Are you telling me I don't have the Holy Spirit?"

"No, I'd never tell anyone that," I respond. Every Christian has the right and the authority of the Holy Spirit, but we impose a limit on what we can experience because of our intellectual understanding or perhaps a fear."

One minister in the Church of Christ, whom I'd known a long time, said, "Well, I've asked God that if this experience you have is real, to let me have it, and it hasn't happened. This makes me feel that it isn't valid."

"I understand that," I said.

He went on, "Still, I'll tell you, I did have an experience the other night that was unusual for me. I woke up in the middle of the night, and I was wide-awake, more than I am at this moment. I've never been so instantly alert in the middle of the night. My wife was sound asleep, and I knew that the only person who knew I was awake was the Lord. So I just lay there. I looked up and just said, 'Lord, I love you. I love you.' I began to weep. That quiet, intimate moment was so overwhelming that I wept softly for over an hour telling him how much I loved him. My pillow was drenched."

He went on. "I'm not that kind of person, so it was not a usual thing. Was *that* the Holy Spirit?"

I replied, "Was it *you*?" I could tell something had awakened in him. He knew it was unique. He knew that God had dealt with him, that he had experienced something special, but he was still judging his experience by someone else's.

The next night I was asked to pray for a little Japanese man to receive the fullness of the Holy Spirit. He was very disappointed. "I've prayed, but nothing has happened."

"You've asked," I said. "Now, do you think the Lord has said no to you?"

"Well, I haven't experienced anything," he said.

"You mean you haven't had an experience like somebody

else has had—is that what you mean?"

"Well, yeah, I guess so, but you know, there was an unusual thing that happened to me," and he talked about waking up in the middle of the night thinking of a man he hated. He said, "I'm not emotional" (and, of course, he'd been trained all of his life to restrain his emotions), "but I thought of this man whom I had hated all of my life, and suddenly, unaccountably, I felt an affection for him. Then another man flashed in my mind that I didn't like, and again I felt kindly and affectionate toward him. I tried to think of other people I didn't like, and there were many, and I began to love all of them. Was *that* the Holy Spirit?"

And I asked, "Was it *you*?"

I could tell a big burden had lifted from his shoulders. He recognized that God was dealing with him. I added, "Look, God said in Romans 5:5 that the love of God will be shed abroad in our hearts by the Holy Spirit. Where do you think that love came from—yourself?" He began realizing that other things would happen if he would just open up and let God have his way in his life.

Almost the next day, another Church of Christ minister called from Wyoming. He said, "Everyone in my house and everyone in my prayer circle has received the Holy Spirit but me. I don't know what my problem is."

I said, "Well, did you *ask*?"

"Oh, yes," he said, "I've asked."

"You mean you haven't had this prayer language experience?"

"Yeah, yeah. But you know, something strange did happen. It happened in broad daylight. I was praying and thanking the Lord for all of the good things that had happened to me when I became so overjoyed that I started to laugh. I haven't told anybody this because I would have felt like an idiot, but I shook and I laughed and I snickered and I cried, and that went on for about half an hour. *That* wasn't the Holy Spirit, was it?"

"Was it *you*?"

"Look, I've got to go," he said. I could tell he wanted to get off the phone so he could laugh some more!

The unity of the Spirit that we've read about in Ephesians 4 for so long can only be brought about as long as we allow the Holy Spirit to operate individually in men. He draws us all together.

A young girl came to me in Michigan. "I'm doing a report on the Jesus Movement," she said, "and I'm sort of confused and disappointed." I asked why. She replied, "I've been studying this thing for about a year now, and I can't find a headquarters, I can't find any leader, and I can't find any doctrine."

I said, "Honey, you have just named the three things that tell me this is from God. The headquarters is in the individual heart. It started in heaven, in God's own heart, and now he sets up his headquarters in each believer's heart as each heart opens to receive him.

"He gave us his doctrine over two, three, and four thousand years ago, and there's no need for any more doctrine.

"And the leaders? It's got one leader, Jesus himself."

Other times when people have asked me, "What is the Jesus Movement?" I have said, "Jesus moving. That's what it is. It's just a grass-roots human response to the drawing power of Jesus himself."

My mom and dad have been through many of the same things spiritually that I have, not only the wonderful experiences in the Lord, but also the perplexing experiences in the church. As they came into the fullness of the Spirit, they were excused from their church circle. My father is a building contractor, my mother is a registered nurse, and they are just worshiping the Lord all the time.

I was down to Nashville on business. I wanted to watch the then-new "Julie Andrews Hour" which was coming on television that night at nine. After dinner my parents left for church, and I went out on the front porch swing. It was late summer, or early in the fall, still warm and beautiful. As I was swinging, I was thinking about how much the Lord has blessed me in this simple wood-frame house, and was just thanking him for the experiences of my youth and for my parents. I was praying in the Spirit. Then I began singing in the Spirit.

Suddenly I became aware of a chorus of crickets. It startled me so. I stopped. But the crickets kept on singing. And I thought, *They're doing the same thing I'm doing. They're just praising the Lord!* So I just joined in again, and we began to sing together, I don't know for how long, about twenty minutes or so. The crickets and I were just having a joyous time in the Lord, when suddenly they stopped.

I said, "What's the matter, guys?" As I did, I looked at my watch, and it was nine o'clock. I said, "Oh, thank you, God," and went on inside. People will think I'm crazy! But when something like that happens to you personally, and you recognize it as being from the Lord, in harmony with the rest of his creation, you realize that's why any of us live, why anything exists at all—to give glory to God. It's an exhilarating experience.

Recently we were in Oral Roberts' home; I was there to speak at ORU's baccalaureate. He had already gone to bed that night when a man came by, a 46-year-old builder and real-estate developer. He'd been something of a renegade who had run from God all his life, but he had come to Oral's house because he had read my story and had said, "I want what Pat Boone has."

We sat and talked. We read some Scriptures, and he said, "That's what I want." We prayed. He sobbed like a child, this millionaire on his knees before the Lord.

The layman who had brought him and I were praying and rejoicing in the Spirit. The builder turned around and said, "Boy, it sounds like y'all are having fun."

"It is fun," I replied. "Paul says that the fruit of the Spirit is love, joy, peace . . . and we're just rejoicing with you."

"Can I pray like that?" he asked.

"Of course you can," we said. Soon he was praying in the Spirit and rejoicing with us. He was just tingling with the joy of knowing that he was with the Lord himself.

We prayed for a while. Then the layman said, "Boy, you ought to be baptized." We looked out the window at Oral Roberts' pool. It was pouring down rain, but he said, "I'm ready."

I quoted Peter's instructions from the Day of Pentecost: "Each one of you must turn from sin, return to God, and be baptized in the name of Jesus Christ for the forgiveness of your sins; then you also shall receive this gift, the Holy Spirit" (Acts 2:38).

"Dick," I explained, "it seems to me that belief and repentance, or turning to God, takes care of your *future*. Baptism, which is somehow related to the washing away of your sins, takes care of your *past*. And he says, 'You also shall receive . . . the Holy Spirit.' That's for living this life *now*. You have received the Holy Spirit almost immediately, as Cornelius did in Acts 10. And he was baptized the same night . . . ." I got my bathing suit on, and these other guys joined me in Oral Roberts' pool. He was baptized the same hour of the night and went on his way rejoicing. It has a scriptural ring to it, doesn't it? We also prayed for the healing of his body, because he shared with us that he had cancer, and said, "I know my wife's prayers have kept me alive till now."

"From now on, *your* prayers will keep you alive," we said. We were quite sure that the whole thing was wrapped up right there in one package, and Oral Roberts didn't know about it until morning!

People are trying to discover truth in so many ways—the occult, for example. *Time* magazine once put a Satan worshiper on its cover with the title: "Satan Returns." I have

191

news for *Time*. He's never been away. He's just come out into the open more.

So many church people don't even perceive the nature of the battle. When I was meeting with the elders of our congregation prior to our being asked to leave our church in California because of our experiences with the Holy Spirit, I kept saying, "Brethren, how can we really fight the supernatural power of the devil with just our thoughts, our intellect, our minds, and our doctrinal understanding and structure? Even if we supposedly could document the fact that God quit performing his signs and wonders in the first century, there's nothing in the Bible that says Satan stopped *his* signs and wonders. So isn't it sort of an unequal contest?"

One of the elders then replied, "Well, now, there are many folks who think Satan is not really a person but is just the reality of evil in the world, perhaps in the baser tendencies of man."

So the problem became apparent. Here was a fine Christian man, a leader, a teacher, an elder. If he's fuzzy about the reality of Satan, if he's not sure that Satan is a person with a whole hierarchy of demonic beings and, as the Bible calls them, "persons without bodies," then he doesn't perceive the nature of the struggle we are in. That explains why so many Christian laymen today, as well as Christian leaders, suffer all kinds of attacks, tragedies, diseases, and setbacks. They don't even know where these things are coming from! They don't know how to put on the armor and fight.

Paul tells us about it in Ephesians 6:10. "Last of all I want to remind you that your strength must come from the Lord's mighty power within you."

I was on the "Dick Cavett Show" one night with Billy Graham. The three of us had a good discussion, which continued after the show. Dick says frankly that he's an agnostic; he's not sure there really is a God at all. He asked me the same question I've heard him ask religious leaders on the air: "What do you say to the student who said to Freud, 'If there is a God, and if I ever stand before him, I'm going to hold up a piece of cancerous bone and ask "Why?"' " In other words, how can a God permit disease, pestilence, famine, earthquakes, and suffering?

"Let me build a hypothetical case," I responded. "Let's say Henry Ford Sr. brings his son into his office and says, 'Son, I want you to have your own business. I'm going to set you up with a whole new division. It will carry your name, your own budget, your own designers and everything. You're going to run it. I'm willing to help you out when you ask me, but you're on your own. You got that, Edsel?'

"It didn't happen this way, of course, but now let's assume that Edsel says, 'Great.' He goes to work, has his car designed, and everything goes along fine. Then he says, 'I'm not a very good administrator, but I've got a friend who is. He's been in charge of a lot of people, and he runs a big organization of his own. I'm going to ask Gus Hall, chairman of the Communist Party in America, to help me out.'

"Soon the division goes down the tubes and out of business. There's embarrassment, disgrace, and a lot of people are thrown out of work. The name becomes a joke in automotive circles."

Right there I paused a minute, and Dick said, "I get it. You're saying that God created the world. He gave it to man, and man gave it to the devil."

I answered, "You sound like a preacher, Dick."

He said, "Well, I've got to get ready for another show." But he had grasped exactly what had happened.

A friend of mine, a missionary in Thailand, began to talk to a Thai government official about God. The man said, "Look, I don't want to hear about it. There is no God. If there is a God who permits disease, pestilence, famine, earthquakes, and tragedy, I don't want to have anything to do with him."

"All right," said my friend, "there is no God. We agree on

that, right? Now . . . there still are earthquakes, pestilence, famine, disease. Whom shall we blame?"

The Thai official said, "Well, I never thought about that. I guess, well—nature, and man himself."

My friend asked, "Then why must you blame it on God?" That man became a Christian. He realized that we oppose ourselves. It's our disobedience, our separation from God, and our desire to go our own way that set us up for all the problems we face—and give Satan a heyday.

So many people are right up to the edge of entering God's Promised Land. We are exactly like the nation of Israel in the Old Testament. They came right up to it and sent spies into it. The spies came back and said, "Oh, it's great, it's beautiful, it really is the land of promise, but there are giants! We can't go in there. We are as grasshoppers." They focused on themselves instead of on the greatness of God and his promises, and so they backed off.

I did that. When I saw my wife changed by God right before my eyes, I lingered for six months, hanging back, thinking, *Well, it's great, but I'm afraid there are giants in that kingdom.* I remained a grasshopper for six months while Shirley was being transformed.

While in Israel, I stood close to a spot at the River Jordan just above Jericho. It was here that the people of Israel entered the land from the wilderness. The priests were carrying the ark, and as their feet touched the water, it parted so God's people could enter the land of promise and provision. They had wandered around for forty years. Now they entered in.

It was also at this spot that Elisha slapped the water with the coat of Elijah and saw the evidence that he had received a double portion of Elijah's spirit: the water parted and he went through.

Later in time, at this same place in the river, Jesus came to John to be baptized. He received the Holy Spirit without measure; the heavens opened, and God, unable to contain himself, said, "This is my beloved Son; I'm pleased with him."

I realized that we all stand back, looking across at the Promised Land, seeing joy and happiness and power in the lives of other people, but afraid to enter in. We're afraid we'll be thought foolish. When Elisha hit the water, all the sons of the prophets were watching, and he didn't know for sure, until he hit it, if God was with him. What if he would have slapped that water and nothing had happened? All the prophets would have laughed. They'd have come over and patted him on the shoulder and said, "That's okay. There's only one Elijah, you know. Don't worry about it." But when he hit the water, it parted, and God confirmed that he had imparted to Elisha his Spirit.

What if the Israelites had come to the edge of the water, walked in, and begun to float around? What if the water hadn't opened up and stayed open? But they *believed* what God said, they stepped out, the waters opened up and stayed opened, and they went through on dry ground.

In a sense, we all must follow Jesus to that very spot in the Jordan and be willing to be humbled, to be "fools for his sake" in order that we may come into the fullness of his Spirit, his provision, his power, and his protection.

It wasn't easy for a singer. An entertainer's whole stock-in-trade is what people think about him. We're geared to protect our public image. And even though *we* may know—and all of us do, if we'd just be honest—that we're no great shakes, we don't admit it. Any entertainer knows he's just another guy or another woman. The women know how much make-up they have to put on and what they have to go through to be beautiful, glamorous sex symbols. The guys know how they have to work with weights and how they too have to use make-up sometimes. But the facade must be carefully protected, because it's so important what people think.

I'd been trained that way for fifteen years. But I was coming to a point where I needed the power of God in my life. I needed miracles. My wife and I simply didn't love each other anymore. We'd known it for two years. My children had arrived at their teen years and were asking me questions I didn't have answers for. Their respect for me as a father had been greatly damaged. They had seen one Pat Boone at church. (We were always faithful churchgoers, even when they had to prop me up to keep me from falling asleep and rolling right over on the bench.) They'd seen another Pat Boone at home. They'd seen another Pat Boone on television and were wondering how many other Pat Boones there were.

My wife had long ago decided not to ask the real Pat Boone to stand up, because she had decided she didn't like any of them, or all of them put together, I had disillusioned and hurt her so badly. There was no way *I* could rebuild that bridge. And she, as a wife, had not fulfilled all my dreams either.

How do a husband and wife regain the love that's gone? Only a miracle could perform it. How does a father regain the respect of his children after he's lost it? Financial problems were mounting and my career seemed to have lost all meaning and thrust.

It just so happened that at that time in my life I picked up a book, *The Cross and the Switchblade,* about a skinny young preacher from Pennsylvania who went into New York and staked his life over and over again on the proposition that God would perform miracles for those who would put their faith in him. I called Dave Wilkerson after I'd read the book. "Dave, is this story true? All of it?"

"Of course it's true," came the answer.

"Well," I said, "I've got a wild idea. I'd like to make a movie about it."

"You're not the first one. Others have wanted to make a movie of *The Cross and the Switchblade,* but the doors have been shut. We just haven't felt that Hollywood would treat this story properly. We know how they twist things around. I don't know you very well" (Dave was very blunt) "and don't know what Hollywood would do with the story, but I'll tell you what—we'll leave it to the Lord. *Jesus*—" and he's praying! He's in New York and I'm in California, and he's talking to Jesus on the telephone—and not only that, but I knew he was getting through; it had become a hot line! *"Lord, it's your story. If this is how you want it to be told, then cause it to happen. Otherwise we don't want a film of it. If it's not in your will, we'll just wait for your leading on it, in Jesus' name.* Anything else, Pat?"

I'm sitting there numb. I told him we'd be in touch and hung up. I sat there in the pantry of our house in the sunlight and thought, *Boy it would be great if the Christian life could be like that!*

Well, we also met George Otis, and then Harald Bredesen . . . all these people who were leading exciting lives, and even though I was intrigued and attracted to what they had, I still held back. I was still trying to understand it all, and I couldn't.

Meanwhile, Shirley made her commitment. One day she went up to her bedroom, closed the door, and said, "Lord, take me, take over my life; I don't know what you have in store for me, but I'm going to offer you my voice." As she offered him her heart, her voice, herself, without reservation, the Lord took her up on it and began to work with her by his Spirit. He bathed her in love.

Miracles did happen. Our four daughters also came into the fullness of the Spirit. We all said, "Lord, you take over. You fill us. You direct our lives. We're going to offer our voices; we'll sing praises to you. We'll speak and pray with the Spirit, and we'll pray with the understanding. Fill us, take over, be the Baptizer in the Holy Spirit. Have your way with us."

And he revolutionized an entertainer's life.